# Philosophy

**GP 100**

**Anthony J. Celano**

Stonehill College
Philosophy Department

## McGraw-Hill

*A Division of The McGraw-Hill Companies*

**McGraw–Hill Primis**
ISBN–10: 0–39–022744–7
ISBN–13: 978–0–39–022744–7

Text:

Discourses
**Abel**

This book was printed on recycled paper.

**Philosophy**

# http://www.primisonline.com

Copyright ©2010 by The McGraw-Hill Companies, Inc. All rights
reserved. Printed in the United States of America. Except as
permitted under the United States Copyright Act of 1976, no part
of this publication may be reproduced or distributed in any form
or by any means, or stored in a database or retrieval system,
without prior written permission of the publisher.

This McGraw-Hill Primis text may include materials submitted to
McGraw-Hill for publication by the instructor of this course. The
instructor is solely responsible for the editorial content of such
materials.

111   PHLOGEN     ISBN-10: 0-39-022744-7     ISBN-13: 978-0-39-022744-7

# Philosophy

# Contents

# Apology

Plato

Plato was born in Athens in about 428 B.C.E. As a youth he associated with Socrates, a philosopher who constantly challenged fellow Athenians to think about virtue and to improve their souls. Plato's initial interest was in politics, but he soon became disillusioned, especially when, under the democracy that was restored after the rule of the "Thirty Tyrants," Socrates was arrested on false charges of impiety and the corruption of youth, convicted, and condemned to die. After the execution of Socrates, Plato moved to nearby Megara for a time and may have traveled to Egypt. In 388 he visited Italy and the city of Syracuse in Sicily. Returning to Athens, he founded the Academy, a school devoted both to philosophical inquiry and to the philosophically based education of politicians. Plato spent most of his life teaching at the Academy (Aristotle was his most famous student) and writing philosophical works. He made two more trips to Syracuse, in 368 and 361, apparently with the intention of turning the city's ruler, Dionysius the Younger, into a "philosopher-king." (If this was indeed his purpose, he failed.) Plato died in Athens in 347 at the age of eighty-one.

Most of Plato's works are written as conversations between Socrates and one or more interlocutors on some topic concerning morality. His best-known "dialogues" (the name by which his surviving works are known) are the *Euthyphro, Apology, Crito, Phaedo, Meno, Symposium,* and *Republic.*

Our reading here is the *Apology,* Plato's account of the defense speech (*apologia* in Greek; hence the title "Apology") and of the two brief additional speeches Socrates gave at his trial. Since Plato was actually present at the trial, we can be confident that his report is substantially accurate.

In his defense speech, Socrates responds to the accusations of Meletus, Anytus, and Lycon that he corrupts the youth of Athens and is impious. Before addressing these official charges, however, Socrates answers the "older charges"—three long-standing prejudices that arose against him as he tried to fulfill his God-given mission of urging Athenians to care about the good of their souls. He explains to the court (1) that he does not pursue natural science, (2) that he neither professes to be a teacher nor charges fees for his conversations, and (3) that he is wiser than others not because he has positive knowledge, but because he—unlike those he questions in his conversations—knows that he does not know. Socrates then defends himself against the two official charges of the corruption of youth and impiety, without ever claiming to know precisely what corruption or piety is.

The jury of 501 found Socrates guilty by a vote of 280 to 221. In the Athenian legal system, the accuser would propose a penalty and the convicted person would propose a counterpenalty—and the jury would have to choose one or the other. Meletus had proposed death; Socrates, in his second speech, proposes what he considers a fitting penalty for his conduct.

The jury chose the death penalty. In his final speech, Socrates reflects on the manner of his defense and addresses separately those who voted against him and those who voted for acquittal.

▼

From *The Dialogues of Plato,* trans. Benjamin Jowett. 3rd ed., vol. 2. New York: Macmillan, 1892 (updated stylistically).

© The McGraw–Hill Companies, 2004

**[Defense Speech]**

How you, men of Athens, have been affected by my accusers, I cannot tell; but I know that they almost made me forget who I was—so persuasively did they speak. And yet they have hardly uttered a word of truth. But of the many falsehoods they told, there was one that quite amazed me: I mean when they said that you should be upon your guard and not allow yourselves to be deceived by the force of my eloquence. To say this, when they were certain to be detected as soon as I opened my lips and proved myself to be anything but a great speaker, did indeed appear to me most shameless—unless by the force of eloquence they mean the force of truth; for if such is their meaning, I admit that I am eloquent. But in how different a way from theirs! Well, as I was saying, they have scarcely spoken the truth at all; but from me you shall hear the whole truth—not, however, delivered after their manner in a set oration duly ornamented with words and phrases. No, by heaven! But I shall use the words and arguments that occur to me at the moment, for I am confident in the justice of my cause. At my time of life I ought not to be appearing before you, men of Athens, in the character of a juvenile orator—let no one expect it of me. And I must beg of you to grant me a favor: If I defend myself in my accustomed manner and you hear me using the words that I have been in the habit of using in the agora,[1] at the tables of the money changers, or anywhere else, I would ask you not to be surprised and not to interrupt me on this account. For I am more than seventy years of age, and appearing now for the first time in a court of law. I am quite a stranger to the language of the place, and therefore I would have you regard me as if I were really a stranger, whom you would excuse if he spoke in his native tongue and after the fashion of his country. Am I making an unfair request of you? Never mind the manner, which may or may not be good, but think only of the truth of my words and give heed to that. Let the speaker speak truly and the judge decide justly.

First I have to reply to the older charges and to my first accusers, and then I will go on to the later ones. For I have had many accusers who have accused me falsely to you during many years; and I am more afraid of them than of Anytus and his associates, who are dangerous, too, in their own way. But far more dangerous are the others, who began when you were children and took possession of your minds with their falsehoods, telling of one Socrates, a wise man, who speculated about the heaven above and searched into the earth beneath, and made the worse appear the better cause. The disseminators of this tale are the accusers whom I dread; for their hearers are apt to think that such inquirers do not believe in the existence of the gods. These accusers are many, and their charges against me are from long ago and were made by them in the days when you were more credulous than you are now—in childhood, or it may have been in youth—and the cause when heard went by default, for there was none to answer. And hardest of all, I do not know and cannot tell the names of my accusers, except in the chance case of a comic poet.[2] All who have persuaded you from envy and malice—some of them having first convinced themselves—all this class of men are most difficult to deal with; for I cannot have them up here and cross-examine them, and therefore I must simply fight with shadows in my own defense and argue when there is no one who answers. I will ask you then to assume with me, as I was saying, that my opponents are of two kinds: one recent, the other old. And I hope that you will see the propriety of my answering the latter first, for these accusations you heard long before the others, and much oftener.

Well, then, I must make my defense and try to clear away, in a short time, a slander that has lasted a long time. May I succeed, if to succeed be for my good and yours, or likely to avail me in my cause. The task is not an easy one; I quite understand the nature of it. And so, leaving the event with God, in obedience to the law I will now make my defense.

I will begin at the beginning, and ask what is the accusation that has given rise to the slander against me, and in fact has encouraged Meletus to bring this charge against me. Well, what do the slanderers say? They shall be my prosecutors, and I will sum up their words in an affidavit: "Socrates is an evildoer and a curious person who searches into things under the earth and in heaven, and he makes the worse appear the better cause; and he teaches these doctrines to others." Such is the nature of the accusation; it is just what you have yourselves seen in the comedy of Aristophanes, who has introduced a man whom he calls Socrates, going about and saying that he walks in air, and talking a deal of nonsense concerning matters of which I do not pretend to know either much or little[3]—not that I mean to speak disparagingly of anyone who is a student of natural philosophy.[4] I would be very sorry if Meletus could bring so grave a charge against me. But the simple truth is, men of Athens, that I have nothing to do with physical speculations. Very many of those here present are witnesses to the truth of this, and to them I appeal. Speak then, you who have heard me, and tell your neighbors whether any of you have ever known me hold forth in few words or in many upon such matters. And from what they say of this part of the charge you will be able to judge of the truth of the rest.

There is little foundation for the report that I am a teacher and take money; this accusation has no more truth in it than the other. Although, if a man were really able to instruct mankind, to receive money for giving instruction would, in my opinion, be an honor to him. There is Gorgias of Leontini, Prodicus of Ceos, and Hippias of Elis,[5] who go the round of the cities and are able to persuade the young men to leave their own citizens, by whom they might be taught for nothing, and come to them whom they not only pay, but are thankful if they may be allowed to pay them. There is at this time a philosopher from Paros residing in Athens, of whom I have heard, and I came to hear of him in this way: I came across a man who has spent a world of money on the Sophists—Callias, the son of Hipponicus.

© The McGraw–Hill Companies, 2004

And knowing that he had sons, I asked him: "Callias," I said, "if your two sons were foals or calves, there would be no difficulty in finding someone to put over them; we would hire a trainer of horses, or a farmer probably, who would improve and perfect them in their own proper virtue and excellence. But since your sons are human beings, whom are you thinking of placing over them? Is there anyone who understands human and political[6] virtue? You must have thought about the matter, for you have sons. Is there anyone?" "There is," he said. "Who is he?" I asked; "and of what country, and what does he charge?" "Evenus of Paros," he replied; "he is the man, and his charge is five minas." Happy is Evenus, I said to myself, if he really has this wisdom and teaches at such a moderate charge. If I had the same, I would be very proud and conceited; but the truth is that I have no knowledge of the kind.

I dare say, Athenians, that someone among you will reply, "Yes, Socrates, but what is the origin of these accusations that are brought against you? There must have been something strange that you have been doing. All these rumors and this talk about you would never have arisen if you had been like other men. Tell us, then, what is the cause of them, for we do not want to make a hasty judgment." Now I regard this as a fair challenge, and I will try to explain to you the reason why I am called wise and have such an evil fame. Please listen, then. And although some of you may think that I am joking, I declare that I will tell you the entire truth.

Men of Athens, this reputation of mine has come of a certain sort of wisdom that I possess. If you ask me what kind of wisdom, I reply: Wisdom such as may perhaps be attained by man, for to that extent I am inclined to believe that I am wise; whereas the persons of whom I was speaking have a superhuman wisdom, which I may fail to describe, because I do not have it myself—and he who says that I have, speaks falsely and is taking away my character. And here, men of Athens, I must beg you not to interrupt me, even if I seem to say something extravagant. For the word that I will speak is not mine. I will refer you to a witness who is worthy of credit. That witness will be the god of Delphi—he will tell you about my wisdom, if I have any, and of what sort it is. You must have known Chaerephon; he was early a friend of mine, and also a friend of yours, for he shared in the recent exile of the people and returned with you. Well, Chaerephon, as you know, was very impetuous in all his doings, and he went to Delphi and boldly asked the oracle to tell him whether—as I was saying, I must beg you not to interrupt—he asked the oracle to tell him whether anyone was wiser than I was, and the Pythian prophetess[7] answered that there was no man wiser. Chaerephon is dead himself; but his brother, who is in court, will confirm the truth of what I am saying.

Why do I mention this? Because I am going to explain to you why I have such an evil name. When I heard the answer, I said to myself: What can the god mean, and what is the interpretation of his riddle? For I know that I have no wisdom, small or great. What then can he mean when he says that I am the wisest of men? And yet he is a god, and cannot lie; that would be against his nature. After long consideration, I thought of a method of investigating the question. I reflected that if I could only find a man wiser than myself, then I might go to the god with a refutation in my hand. I would say to him, "Here is a man who is wiser than I am; but you said that I was the wisest." Accordingly I went to one who had the reputation of wisdom, and observed him—his name I need not mention; he was a politician whom I selected for examination—and the result was as follows: When I began to talk with him, I could not help thinking that he was not really wise, although he was thought wise by many, and still wiser by himself. And then I tried to explain to him that he thought himself wise, but was not really wise. And the consequence was that he hated me, and his enmity was shared by several who were present and heard me. So I left him, saying to myself as I went away: Well, although I do not suppose that either of us knows anything really beautiful and good, I am better off than he is—for he knows nothing and thinks that he knows, while I neither know nor think that I know. In this one small respect, then, I seem to have the advantage of him. Then I went to another who had still higher pretensions to wisdom, and my conclusion was exactly the same. And so I made another enemy of him, and of many others besides him.

Then I went to one man after another, being not unconscious of the enmity that I provoked, and I lamented and feared this. But necessity was laid upon me: The word of God, I thought, ought to be considered first. And I said to myself: I must go to all who appear to know, and find out the meaning of the oracle. And I swear to you, Athenians, by the dog I swear—for I must tell you the truth—the result of my mission was just this: I found that the men most in repute were all but the most foolish; and that others less esteemed were really wiser and better. I will tell you the tale of my wanderings and of the Herculean labors, so to speak, that I endured only to find at last the oracle irrefutable. After the politicians, I went to the poets—tragic, dithyrambic, and all sorts. And there, I said to myself, you will be instantly detected; now you will find out that you are more ignorant than they are. Accordingly, I took them some of the most elaborate passages in their own writings and asked what was the meaning of them—thinking that they would teach me something. Will you believe me? I am almost ashamed to confess the truth, but I must say that there is hardly a person present who would not have talked better about their poetry than they did themselves. Then I knew that not by wisdom do poets write poetry, but by a sort of genius and inspiration; they are like seers or prophets, who also say many fine things but do not understand the meaning of them. The poets appeared to me to be much in the same case. And I further observed that upon the strength of their poetry they believed themselves to be the wisest of men in other things in which they were not wise. So I departed, conceiving myself to be superior to them for the same reason that I was superior to the politicians.

© The McGraw–Hill Companies, 2004

At last I went to the artisans, for I was conscious that I knew nothing at all, as I may say, and I was sure that they knew many fine things. And here I was not mistaken, for they did know many things of which I was ignorant, and in this they certainly were wiser than I was. But I observed that even the good artisans fell into the same error as the poets: Because they were good workmen, they thought that they also knew all sorts of high matters; and this defect in them overshadowed their wisdom. And therefore I asked myself on behalf of the oracle, whether I would like to be as I was, neither having their knowledge nor their ignorance, or like them in both. And I answered to myself and to the oracle that I was better off as I was.

This inquiry has led to my having many enemies of the worst and most dangerous kind, and has given occasion also to many calumnies. And I am called wise, for my hearers always imagine that I myself possess the wisdom that I find lacking in others. But the truth is, men of Athens, that only God is wise; and by his answer he intends to show that the wisdom of men is worth little or nothing. He is not speaking of Socrates; he is only using my name by way of illustration, as if he said: He is the wisest, who, like Socrates, knows that his wisdom is in truth worth nothing. And so I go about the world, obedient to the god, and search and inquire into the wisdom of anyone, whether citizen or stranger, who appears to be wise. And if he is not wise, then in vindication of the oracle I show him that he is not wise. And my occupation quite absorbs me, and I have no time to give either to any public matter of interest or to any concern of my own, but I am in utter poverty by reason of my devotion to the god.

There is another thing: Young men of the richer classes, who do not have much to do, come around me of their own accord. They like to hear the pretenders examined, and they often imitate me and proceed to examine others. There are plenty of persons, as they quickly discover, who think that they know something but really know little or nothing. And then those who are examined by them, instead of being angry with themselves, are angry with me. "This confounded Socrates," they say; "this villainous misleader of youth!" And then if somebody asks them, "Why, what evil does he practice or teach?," they do not know, and cannot say. But in order that they may not appear to be at a loss, they repeat the ready-made charges that are used against all philosophers about teaching things up in the clouds and under the earth, having no gods, and making the worse appear the better cause. For they do not like to confess that their pretense of knowledge has been detected—which is the truth. And as they are numerous and ambitious and energetic, and are drawn up in battle array and have persuasive tongues, they have filled your ears with their loud and inveterate calumnies. And this is the reason why my three accusers, Meletus and Anytus and Lycon, have set upon me: Meletus, who has a quarrel with me on behalf of the poets; Anytus, on behalf of the craftsmen and politicians; and Lycon, on behalf of the rhetoricians. And as I said at the beginning, I cannot expect to get rid of such a mass of calumny all in a moment. And this, men of Athens, is the truth and the whole truth; I have concealed nothing, I have dissembled nothing. And yet I know that my plainness of speech makes them hate me—and what is their hatred but a proof that I am speaking the truth? Hence the prejudice has arisen against me, and this is the reason for it, as you will find out either in this or in any future inquiry.

I have said enough in my defense against the first class of my accusers; I turn now to the second class. They are headed by Meletus, that good man and true lover of his country, as he calls himself. Against these, too, I must try to make a defense. Let their affidavit be read. It contains something of this kind: It says that Socrates is a doer of evil who corrupts the youth; and that he does not believe in the gods of the state, but has other new divinities of his own. Such is the charge. And now let us examine the particular counts. He says that I am a doer of evil and corrupt the youth. But I say, men of Athens, that Meletus is a doer of evil, in that he pretends to be in earnest when he is only in jest, and is so eager to bring men to trial from a pretended zeal and interest about matters in which he really never had the smallest interest. And the truth of this I will try to prove to you.

Come here, Meletus, and let me ask you a question. Do you think a great deal about the improvement of youth?

Yes, I do.

Tell the judges, then, who is their improver—for you must know, as you have taken the pains to discover their corrupter, and are citing and accusing me before them. Speak, then, and tell the judges who their improver is. . . . Observe, Meletus, that you are silent and have nothing to say. But is not this rather disgraceful, and a very considerable proof of what I was saying, that you have no interest in the matter? Speak up, friend, and tell us who their improver is.

The laws.

But that, my good sir, is not my meaning. I want to know who the *person* is who, in the first place, knows the laws.

The judges, Socrates, who are present in court.

What, do you mean to say, Meletus, that they are able to instruct and improve youth?

Certainly they are.

All of them, or some only and not others?

All of them.

By the goddess Hera, that is good news! There are plenty of improvers, then. And what do you say of the audience? Do they improve them?

Yes, they do.

And the senators?

© The McGraw–Hill
Companies, 2004

Yes, the senators improve them.

But perhaps the members of the assembly corrupt them? Or do they too improve them?

They improve them.

Then every Athenian improves and elevates them—all, with the exception of myself; I alone am their corrupter. Is that what you affirm?

That is what I stoutly affirm.

I am very unfortunate if you are right. But suppose I ask you a question: How about horses? Does one man do them harm, and everyone else does them good? Is not the exact opposite the truth? One man is able to do them good, or at least not many. The trainer of horses, that is to say, does them good, and others who have to do with them injure them. Is not that true, Meletus, of horses, or of any other animals? Most assuredly it is, whether you and Anytus say yes or no. Happy indeed would be the condition of youth if they had one corrupter only, and all the rest of the world were their improvers. But you, Meletus, have sufficiently shown that you never had a thought about the young. Your carelessness is seen in your not caring about the very things that you bring against me.

And now, Meletus, I will ask you another question—by Zeus I will: Which is better, to live among bad citizens, or among good ones? Answer, friend, I say; the question is one that may be easily answered. Do not the good do their neighbors good, and the bad do them evil?

Certainly.

And is there anyone who would rather be injured than benefited by those who live with him? Answer, my good friend; the law requires you to answer. Does anyone like to be injured?

Certainly not.

And when you accuse me of corrupting the youth making them worse, do you allege that I corrupt them intentionally or unintentionally?

Intentionally, I say.

But you have just admitted that the good do their neighbors good, and evil do them evil. Now, is that a truth that your superior wisdom has recognized thus early in life, and am I, at my age, in such darkness and ignorance as not to know that if a man with whom I have to live is corrupted by me, I am very likely to be harmed by him? And yet I corrupt him, and intentionally, too? So you say, although neither I nor any other human being is ever likely to be convinced by you. But either I do not corrupt them, or I corrupt them unintentionally; and on either view of the case you lie. If my offense is unintentional, the law has no cognizance of unintentional offenses; you ought to have taken me privately, and warned and admonished me. For if I had been better advised, I would have stopped doing what I only did unintentionally—no doubt I would have. But you had nothing to say to me and refused to teach me. And now you bring me up in this court, which is a place not of instruction, but of punishment.

It will be very clear to you, Athenians, as I was saying, that Meletus has no care at all, great or small, about the matter. But still I should like to know, Meletus, in what I am affirmed to corrupt the young. I suppose you mean, as I infer from your indictment, that I teach them not to acknowledge the gods that the state acknowledges, but some other new divinities or spiritual agencies instead. These are the lessons by which I corrupt the youth, as you say.

Yes, that I say emphatically.

Then, by the gods, Meletus (of whom we are speaking), tell me and the court, in somewhat plainer terms, what you mean. For I do not as yet understand whether you affirm that I teach other men to acknowledge some gods, and therefore that I do believe in gods, and am not an entire atheist. This you do not lay to my charge, but you only say that they are not the same gods that the city recognizes; the charge is that they are different gods. Or do you mean that I am an atheist simply, and a teacher of atheism?

I mean the latter—that you are a complete atheist.

What an extraordinary statement! Why do you think so, Meletus? Do you mean that I do not believe in the godhead of the sun or moon, like other men?

I assure you, judges, that he does not; for he says that the sun is stone, and the moon earth.

Friend Meletus, you think that you are accusing Anaxagoras;[8] and you have a bad opinion of the judges, if you think them so illiterate as not to know that these doctrines are found in the books of Anaxagoras of Clazomenae, which are full of them. And so, indeed, the youth are said to be taught these doctrines by Socrates, when there are not unfrequently exhibitions of them at the theater (price of admission one drachma at the most), and they might pay their money and laugh at Socrates if he pretends to father these extraordinary views. And so, Meletus, do you really think that I do not believe in any god?

I swear by Zeus that you believe absolutely in none at all.

Nobody will believe you, Meletus, and I am pretty sure that you do not believe yourself. I cannot help thinking, men of Athens, that Meletus is reckless and impudent, and that he has written this indictment in a spirit of mere wantonness and youthful bravado. He has compounded a riddle, thinking to test me. He said to himself: I shall see whether the wise Socrates will discover my facetious contradiction, or whether I shall be able to deceive him and the rest of them. For he certainly does appear to me to contradict himself in the indictment as much as if he said that Socrates is guilty of not believing in the gods, and yet of believing in them—but this is not like a person who is in earnest.

I would like you, men of Athens, to join me in examining what I conceive to be his inconsistency; and you, Meletus, answer. And I must remind the audience of my request that they not make a disturbance if I speak in my accustomed manner.

Meletus, did anyone ever believe in the existence of human things, and not of human beings? . . . I wish, men of Athens, that he would answer, and not be always trying to get up an interruption. Did ever any man believe in horsemanship, and not in horses? Or in flute-playing, and not in flute players? No, my friend; I will answer to you and to the court, since you refuse to answer for yourself. There is no man who ever did. But now please to answer the next question: Can a man believe in spiritual and divine agencies, and not in spirits or demigods?

He cannot.

How lucky I am to have extracted that answer, by the assistance of the court! But then you swear in the indictment that I teach and believe in divine or spiritual agencies (whether new or old). At any rate, I believe in spiritual agencies—so you say and swear in the affidavit. And yet if I believe in divine beings, how can I help believing in spirits or demigods? To be sure, I must; and therefore I may assume that your silence gives consent. Now what are spirits or demigods? Are they not either gods or the sons of gods?

Certainly they are.

But this is what I call the facetious riddle you have invented: The demigods or spirits are gods, and you say first that I do not believe in gods, and then again that I do believe in gods—that is, if I believe in demigods. For if the demigods are the illegitimate sons of gods—whether by the nymphs or by any other mothers of whom they are said to be the sons—what human being will ever believe that there are no gods if they are the sons of gods? You might as well affirm the existence of mules, and deny that of horses and asses. Such nonsense, Meletus, could only have been intended by you to test me. You have put this into the indictment because you had nothing real of which to accuse me. But no one who has a particle of understanding will ever be convinced by you that the same men can believe in divine and superhuman things, and yet not believe that there are gods and demigods and heroes.

I have said enough in answer to the charge of Meletus; any elaborate defense is unnecessary. But I know only too well how many are the enmities that I have incurred, and this is what will be my destruction if I am destroyed—not Meletus or Anytus, but the envy and detraction of the world, which has been the death of many good men, and will probably be the death of many more; there is no danger of my being the last of them.

Someone will say: Are you not ashamed, Socrates, of a course of life that is likely to bring you to an untimely end? To him I may fairly answer: There you are mistaken. A man who is good for anything ought not to calculate the chance of living or dying; he ought only to consider whether in doing anything he is doing right or wrong—acting the part of a good man or of a bad. But, upon your view, the heroes who fell at Troy were not good for much, and the son of Thetis above all, who altogether despised danger in comparison with disgrace.[9] And when he was so eager to slay Hector, his goddess mother said to him, that if he avenged his companion Patroclus and slew Hector, he would die himself. "Fate," she said, in these or similar words, "waits for you next after Hector." Receiving this warning, he utterly despised danger and death, and instead of fearing them, feared rather to live in dishonor and not to avenge his friend. "Let me die at once," he replied, "and be avenged of my enemy, rather than abide here by the beaked ships, a laughing stock and a burden to the earth." Had Achilles any thought of death and danger? For wherever a man's place is, whether the place which he has chosen or that in which he has been placed by a commander, there he ought to remain in the hour of danger; he should not think of death or of anything but of disgrace. And this, men of Athens, is a true saying.

My conduct would be very strange, men of Athens, if I who, when I was ordered by the generals whom you chose to command me at Potidaea and Amphipolis and Delium, remained where they placed me, like any other man, facing death—if now, when, as I conceive and imagine, God orders me to fulfill the philosopher's mission of searching into myself and other men, I were to desert my post through fear of death, or any other fear. That would indeed be strange, and I might justly be arraigned in court for denying the existence of the gods, if I disobeyed the oracle because I was afraid of death, thinking that I was wise when I was not wise. For the fear of death is indeed the pretense of wisdom and not real wisdom, being a pretense of knowing the unknown. No one knows whether death, which men in their fear apprehend to be the greatest evil, may not be the greatest good. Is not this ignorance of a disgraceful sort, the ignorance of thinking that one knows what one does not know? And in this respect only I believe myself to differ from men in general, and may perhaps claim to be wiser than they are—that whereas I know but little of the world below, I do not suppose that I know. But I do know that injustice and disobedience to a better, whether God or man, is evil and dishonorable, and I will never fear or avoid a possible good rather than a certain evil. And therefore if you let me go now, and are not convinced by Anytus, who said that since I had been prosecuted I must be put to death (or, if not, that I ought never to have been prosecuted at all), and that if I escape now, your sons will all be utterly ruined by listening to my words— if you say to me, Socrates, this time we will not mind Anytus, and you will be let off, but upon one condition, that you are not to inquire and speculate in this way any more, and that if you are caught doing so again you shall die—if this were the condition on which you let me go, I would reply: Men of Athens, I honor and love you; but I shall obey God rather than you, and while I have life and strength I shall never cease from the

© The McGraw–Hill Companies, 2004

practice and teaching of philosophy, exhorting anyone whom I meet and saying to him after my manner: You, my friend—a citizen of the great and mighty and wise city of Athens—are you not ashamed of heaping up the greatest amount of money and honor and reputation, and caring so little about wisdom and truth and the greatest improvement of the soul, which you never regard or heed at all? And if the person with whom I am arguing says, "Yes, I do care," then I do not leave him or let him go at once, but I proceed to interrogate and examine and cross-examine him. And if I think that he has no virtue in him, but only says that he has, I reproach him with undervaluing the greater and overvaluing the less. And I shall repeat the same words to everyone whom I meet, young and old, citizen and alien, but especially to the citizens, since they are my brethren. For know that this is the command of God, and I believe that no greater good has ever happened in the state than my service to the God. For I do nothing but go about persuading you all, old and young alike, not to take thought for your persons or your properties, but first and chiefly to care about the greatest improvement of the soul. I tell you that virtue is not given by money, but that from virtue comes money and every other good of man, public as well as private. This is my teaching, and if this is the doctrine that corrupts the youth, I am a mischievous person. But if anyone says that this is not my teaching, he is speaking an untruth. Therefore, men of Athens, I say to you, do as Anytus bids or not as Anytus bids, and either acquit me or not; but whichever you do, understand that I shall never alter my ways, not even if I have to die many times.

Men of Athens, do not interrupt, but hear me; there was an understanding between us that you should hear me to the end. I have something more to say, at which you may be inclined to cry out. But I believe that to hear me will be good for you, and therefore I beg that you will not cry out. I would have you know that if you kill such a one as I am, you will injure yourselves more than you will injure me. Neither Meletus nor Anytus can injure me, for a bad man is not permitted to injure someone better than himself. I do not deny that Anytus may, perhaps, kill me, or drive me into exile or deprive me of civil rights. And he may imagine, and others may imagine, that he is inflicting a great injury upon me; but there I do not agree. For the evil of doing as he is doing—the evil of unjustly taking away the life of another—is greater far.

And now, Athenians, I am not going to argue for my own sake, as you may think, but for yours, that you may not sin against God by condemning me, who am his gift to you. For if you kill me you will not easily find a successor to me, who, if I may use such a ludicrous figure of speech, am a sort of gadfly[10] given to the state by God; and the state is a great and noble steed who is tardy in his motions owing to his very size, and requires to be stirred into life. I am that gadfly that God has attached to the state, and all day long and in all places am always fastening upon you, arousing and persuading and reproaching you. You will not easily find another like me, and therefore I would advise you to spare me. I dare say that you may feel out of temper (like a person who is suddenly awakened from sleep), and you think that you might easily strike me dead as Anytus advises. And then you would sleep on for the remainder of your lives, unless God in his care of you sent you another gadfly. When I say that I am given to you by God, the proof of my mission is this: If I had been like other men, I would not have neglected all my own concerns or patiently seen the neglect of them during all these years, while attending to your concerns—coming to you individually like a father or older brother, exhorting you to regard virtue. Such conduct, I say, would be unlike human nature. If I had gained anything, or if my exhortations had been paid, there would have been some sense in my doing so. But now, as you will perceive, not even the impudence of my accusers dares to say that I have ever exacted or sought pay of anyone—of that they have no witness. And I have a sufficient witness to the truth of what I say: my poverty.

Someone may wonder why I go about in private giving advice and busying myself with the concerns of others, but do not venture to come forward in public and advise the state. I will tell you why. You have heard me speak at many times and in various places of an oracle or sign that comes to me, and is the divinity that Meletus ridicules in the indictment. This sign, which is a kind of voice, first began to come to me when I was a child. It always forbids but never commands me to do anything that I am going to do. This is what deters me from being a politician. And rightly, I think. For I am certain, men of Athens, that if I had engaged in politics, I would have perished long ago, and done no good either to you or to myself. And do not be offended at my telling you the truth—for the truth is that no man who goes to war with you or any other multitude, honestly striving against the many lawless and unrighteous deeds that are done in a state, will save his life. He who will fight for the right, if he would live even for a brief space, must have a private station and not a public one.

I can give you convincing evidence of what I say, not words only, but what you value far more—actions. Let me relate to you an incident from my own life that will prove to you that I would never have yielded to injustice from any fear of death, and that if I had refused to yield, I would have died at once. I will tell you a tale of the courts, not very interesting perhaps, but nevertheless true. The only office of state that I ever held, men of Athens, was that of senator. The tribe Antiochis, which is my tribe, had the presidency at the trial of the generals who had not taken up the bodies of the slain after the battle of Arginusae; and you proposed to try them in a body, contrary to law, as you all thought afterwards. But at the time I was the only one of the prytanes[11] who was opposed to the illegality, and I gave my vote against you. And when the orators threatened to impeach and arrest me, and you called and shouted, I made up my mind

© The McGraw–Hill Companies, 2004

that I would run the risk, having law and justice with me, rather than take part in your injustice because I feared imprisonment and death. This happened in the days of the democracy. But when the oligarchy of the Thirty was in power, they sent for me and four others into the rotunda, and ordered us to bring Leon the Salaminian from Salamis, because they wanted to put him to death. This is an example of the sort of commands that they were always giving with the view of implicating as many as possible in their crimes. And then I showed, not in word only but in deed, that (if I may be allowed to use such an expression) I cared not a straw for death, and that my great and only care was that I should not do an unjust or unholy thing. For the strong arm of that oppressive power did not frighten me into doing wrong. And when we came out of the rotunda the other four went to Salamis and fetched Leon, but I went quietly home—for which I might have lost my life, had not the power of the Thirty shortly afterwards come to an end. And many will witness to my words.

Now do you really imagine that I could have survived all these years, if I had led a public life, supposing that like a good man I had always maintained the right and had made justice, as I ought, the first thing? No indeed, men of Athens, neither I nor any other man. But I have been always the same in all my actions, public as well as private, and I never have yielded any base compliance to those who are slanderously termed my disciples, or to any other persons. Not that I have any regular disciples. But if anyone likes to come and hear me while I am pursuing my mission, whether he be young or old, he is not excluded. Nor do I converse only with those who pay; but anyone, whether he be rich or poor, may ask and answer me and listen to my words. And whether he turns out to be a bad man or a good one, neither result can be justly imputed to me, for I never taught or professed to teach him anything. And if anyone says that he has ever learned or heard anything from me in private that all the world has not heard, let me tell you that he is lying.

But I will be asked: Why do people delight in continually conversing with you? I have told you already, Athenians, the whole truth about this matter: They like to hear the cross-examination of the pretenders to wisdom; there is amusement in it. Now this duty of cross-examining other men has been imposed upon me by God and has been signified to me by oracles, visions, and in every way in which the will of divine power was ever intimated to anyone. This is true, Athenians—or, if not true, would be soon refuted. If I am or have been corrupting the youth, those of them who are now grown up and become aware that I gave them bad advice in the days of their youth should come forward as accusers and take their revenge. Or, if they do not like to come themselves, some of their relatives, fathers, brothers, or other kinsmen should say what evil their families have suffered at my hands. Now is the time. Many of them I see in the court. There is Crito, who is of the same age and of the same deme[12] as myself, and there is Critobulus, his son, whom I also see. Then again there is Lysanias of Sphettus, who is the father of Aeschines—he is present. And also there is Antiphon of Cephisus, who is the father of Epigenes, and there are the brothers of several who have associated with me. There is Nicostratus, the son of Theosdotides and the brother of Theodotus (Theodotus himself is now dead, and therefore he, at any rate, will not seek to stop him). And there is Paralus, the son of Demodocus, who had a brother Theages; and Adeimantus the son of Ariston, whose brother Plato is present; and Aeantodorus, who is the brother of Apollodorus, whom I also see. I might mention a great many others, some of whom Meletus should have produced as witnesses in the course of his speech; and let him still produce them, if he has forgotten—I will make way for him. And let him say, if he has any testimony of the sort which he can produce. No, Athenians, the very opposite is the truth. For all these are ready to witness on behalf of the corrupter, of the injurer of their kindred, as Meletus and Anytus call me—not the corrupted youth only (there might have been a motive for that) but their uncorrupted older relatives. Why should they too support me with their testimony? Why, indeed, except for the sake of truth and justice, and because they know that I am speaking the truth and that Meletus is a liar?

Well, Athenians, this and things like this is all the defense that I have to offer. Yet a word more. There may be someone who is offended by me, when he calls to mind how he himself on a similar, or even a less serious occasion, prayed and entreated the judges with many tears, and how he produced his children in court, which was a moving spectacle, together with a host of relations and friends—whereas I, who am probably in danger of my life, will do none of these things. The contrast may occur to his mind, and he may be set against me, and vote in anger because he is displeased at me on this account. Now if there be such a person among you—I do not say that there is—to him I may fairly reply: My friend, I am a man, and like other men, a creature of flesh and blood, and not "of wood or stone," as Homer says.[13] And I have a family, yes, and sons, Athenians, three in number—one almost a man, and two others who are still young. And yet I will not bring any of them here in order to petition you for an acquittal. And why not? Not from any self-assertion or lack of respect for you. Whether I am or am not afraid of death is another question, of which I will not now speak. But, having regard to public opinion, I feel that such conduct would be discreditable to myself, to you, and to the whole state. One who has reached my years, and who has a name for wisdom, should not demean himself. Whether this opinion of me is deserved or not, at any rate the world has decided that Socrates is in some way superior to other men. And if those among you who are said to be superior in wisdom and courage, and any other virtue, demean themselves in this way, how shameful is their conduct! I have seen men of reputation, when they have been condemned, behaving in the strangest manner: They seemed to think that they were going to suffer something dreadful if they died, and that they could be immortal if you only allowed them to live. And I think that such are a dishonor to the state, and that any stranger coming in would have said of them that the most eminent men of Athens, to whom the Athenians themselves give honor and command, are no better than women. And I say that these things ought not to be done by those of us who have a reputation. And if they are done, you ought not to permit them; you ought rather to show that you are far more disposed to condemn the man who gets up a doleful scene and makes the city ridiculous, than him who holds his peace.

But, setting aside the question of public opinion, there seems to be something wrong in asking a favor of a judge and thus procuring an acquittal, instead of informing and convincing him. For his duty is not to make a present of justice, but to give judgment; and he has sworn that he will judge according to the laws, and not according to his own good pleasure. And we ought not to encourage you, nor should you allow yourself to be encouraged, in this habit of perjury—there can be no piety in that. Do not then require me to do what I consider dishonorable and impious and wrong, especially now, when I am being tried for impiety on the indictment of Meletus. For if, men of Athens, by force of persuasion and entreaty I could overpower your oaths, then I would be teaching you to believe that there are no gods, and in defending myself I would simply convict myself of the charge of not believing in them. But that is not so—far otherwise. For I do believe that there are gods, and in a sense higher than that in which any of my accusers believe in them. And to you and to God I commit my cause, to determine what is best for you and for me.

**[Counter-Penalty Speech]**

There are many reasons why I am not grieved, men of Athens, at the vote of condemnation. I expected it, and am only surprised that the votes are so nearly equal—for I had thought that the majority against me would have been far larger. But if thirty votes had gone over to the other side, I would have been acquitted. And I may say, I think, that I have escaped Meletus. I may say more: Without the assistance of Anytus and Lycon, anyone can see that he would not have had a fifth part of the votes, as the law requires, in which case he would have incurred a fine of a thousand drachmas.

The man proposes death as the penalty. And what shall I propose on my part, men of Athens? Clearly that which is my due. And what is my due? What return shall be made to the man who has never had the sense to be idle during his whole life, but has been careless of what the many care for—wealth, family interests, military offices, speaking in the assembly, magistracies, plots, and political parties? Reflecting that I was really too honest a man to be a politician and live, I did not go where I could do no good to you or to myself. But where I could do the greatest good privately to every one of you—that is where I went, and sought to persuade every man among you that he must look to himself, and seek virtue and wisdom before he looks to his private interests, and look to the state itself before he looks to the interests of the state; and that this should be the order that he observes in all his actions. What shall be done to such a person? Doubtless some good thing, men of Athens, if he has his reward; and the good should be of a kind suitable to him. What would be a reward suitable to a poor man who is your benefactor, and who desires leisure that he may instruct you? There can be no reward so fitting as maintenance in the Prytaneum,[14] men of Athens—a reward that he deserves far more than the citizen who has won the prize at Olympia in the horse or chariot race, whether the chariots were drawn by two horses or by many. For I am in need, and he has enough; and he only gives you the appearance of happiness, and I give you the reality. And if I am to estimate the penalty fairly, I would say that maintenance in the Prytaneum is the just return.

Perhaps you think that I am arrogant in what I am saying now, as in what I said before about the tears and prayers. But this is not so. I speak rather because I am convinced that I never intentionally wronged anyone, although I cannot convince you—the time has been too short. If there were a law at Athens, as there is in other cities, that a capital case should not be decided in one day, then I believe that I would have convinced you. But I cannot in a moment refute great slanders; and, as I am convinced that I never wronged another, I will assuredly not wrong myself. I will not say of myself that I deserve any evil, or propose any penalty. Why should I? Because I am afraid of the penalty of death that Meletus proposes? When I do not know whether death is a good or an evil, why should I propose a penalty that would certainly be an evil? Shall I say imprisonment? And why should I live in prison and be the slave of the magistrates of the year—of the Eleven? Or shall the penalty be a fine, and imprisonment until the fine is paid? There is the same objection. I would have to lie in prison, for I have no money and cannot pay. And if I say exile (and this may possibly be the penalty that you will assign), I must indeed be blinded by the love of life, if I am so irrational as to expect that when you, who are my fellow citizens, cannot endure my discourses and words, and have found them so grievous and odious that you will have no more of them, others are likely to endure me. No indeed, men of Athens, that is not very likely. And what kind of life would I lead, at my age, wandering from city to city, ever changing my place of exile, and always being driven out? For I am quite sure that wherever I go, there as here, the young men will flock to me; and if I drive them away, their elders will drive me out at their request; and if I let them come, their fathers and friends will drive me out for their sakes.

© The McGraw–Hill Companies, 2004

Someone will say: Yes, Socrates, but cannot you hold your tongue? And then you could go into a foreign city and no one would interfere with you. Now I have great difficulty in making you understand my answer to this. For if I tell you that to do as you say would be a disobedience to God, and therefore that I cannot hold my tongue, you will not believe that I am serious; and if I say again that daily to discourse about virtue, and of those other things about which you hear me examining myself and others, is the greatest good of man, and that the unexamined life is not worth living, you are still less likely to believe me. Yet I say what is true, although a thing of which it is hard for me to persuade you. Also, I have never been accustomed to think that I deserve to suffer any harm. If I had money, I might have assessed a penalty of what I was able to pay, and not have been harmed. But I have no money, and therefore I must ask you to proportion the fine to my means. Well, perhaps I could afford a mina, and therefore I propose that penalty. Plato, Crito, Critobulus, and Apollodorus, my friends here, bid me say thirty minas, and they will be the sureties. Let thirty minas be the penalty, for which sum they will be ample security to you.

**[Final Speech]**

Not much time will be gained, Athenians, in return for the evil name that you will get from the detractors of the city, who will say that you killed Socrates, a wise man—for they will call me wise, even though I am not wise, when they want to reproach you. If you had waited a little while, your desire would have been fulfilled in the course of nature. For I am far advanced in years, as you may perceive, and not far from death. I am speaking now not to all of you, but only to those who have condemned me to death. And I have another thing to say to them: You think that I was convicted because I had no words of the sort that would have procured my acquittal—I mean, if I had thought fit to leave nothing undone or unsaid. Not so; the deficiency that led to my conviction was not of words—certainly not. But I did not have the boldness or impudence or inclination to address you as you would have liked me to do, weeping and wailing and lamenting, and saying and doing many things which you have been accustomed to hear from others, and which, as I maintain, are unworthy of me. I thought at the time that I ought not to do anything servile when in danger. Nor do I now regret of the style of my defense; I would rather die having spoken after my manner, than speak in your manner and live. For neither in war nor in court ought I or any man to use every way of escaping death. Often in battle there can be no doubt that if a man will throw away his arms and fall on his knees before his pursuers, he may escape death. And in other dangers there are other ways of escaping death, if a man is willing to say and do anything. The difficulty, my friends, is not to avoid death, but to avoid wickedness; for wickedness runs faster than death. I am old and move slowly, and the slower runner has overtaken me. My accusers are keen and quick, and the faster runner, wickedness, has overtaken them. And now I depart condemned by you to suffer the penalty of death; they too go their ways condemned by the truth to suffer the penalty of villainy and wrong. And I must abide by my award; let them abide by theirs. I suppose that these things may be regarded as fated—and I think they are fitting.

And now, men who have condemned me, I wish to prophesy to you. For I am about to die, and in the hour of death men are gifted with prophetic power. And I prophesy to you who are my murderers that, immediately after my departure, a punishment far heavier than the punishment of death that you have inflicted on me will surely await you. You have killed me because you wanted to escape the accuser, and not to give an account of your lives. But that will not be as you suppose; far otherwise. For I say that you will have more accusers than you have now—accusers whom until now I have restrained. And since they are younger they will be more inconsiderate with you, and you will be more offended at them. If you think that by killing men you can prevent someone from censuring your evil lives, you are mistaken—that is not a way of escape that is either possible or honorable. The easiest and the noblest way is not to cut down others, but to improve yourselves. This is the prophecy that I utter before my departure to the judges who have condemned me.

You who would have acquitted me, I would like also to talk with you about what has come to pass, while the magistrates are busy and before I go to the place where I must die. Stay with me this little while, for we may as well talk with one another while there is time. You are my friends, and I would like to show you the meaning of this event that has happened to me. My judges—for you I may truly call judges—I would like to tell you of something remarkable. Until now, the divine faculty of which the internal oracle is the source has constantly been in the habit of opposing me even about trifles, if I was going to make a slip or error in any matter. And now, as you see, there has come upon me that which may be thought, and is generally believed to be, the last and worst evil. But the oracle made no sign of opposition, either when I was leaving my house in the morning, or when I was on my way to the court, or while I was speaking, at anything that I was going to say. I have often been stopped in the middle of a speech, but now in nothing I either said or did regarding the matter in hand has the oracle opposed me. What do I take to be the explanation of this silence? I will tell you. It is an intimation that what has happened to me is a good, and that those of us who think that death is an evil are in error. For the customary sign would surely have opposed me had I been going to evil and not to good.

Let us reflect in another way, and we will see that there is great reason to hope that death is a good. For death is one of two things: either a state

© The McGraw–Hill Companies, 2004

of nothingness and utter unconsciousness; or, as men say, a change and migration of the soul from this world to another. Now if you suppose that there is no consciousness, but a sleep like the sleep of him who is undisturbed even by dreams, death will be an unspeakable gain. For if a person were to select the night in which his sleep was undisturbed even by dreams, and were to compare with this the other days and nights of his life, and then were to tell us how many days and nights he had passed in the course of his life better and more pleasantly than this one, I think that any man—not only a private man, but even the great king[15]—would find few such days or nights, in comparison with the others. Now if death be of such a nature, I say that to die is gain; for eternity is then only a single night. But if death is the journey to another place, and there, as men say, all the dead abide, what good, my friends and judges, can be greater than this? If indeed, when the pilgrim arrives in the world below, he is delivered from those who claim to be judges in this world, and finds the true judges who are said to give judgment there—Minos and Rhadamanthus, Aeacus and Triptolemus, and other sons of God who were just in their own life—that pilgrimage will be worth making. What would not a man give if he might converse with Orpheus and Musaeus, Hesiod and Homer? Indeed, if this be true, let me die again and again. I myself, too, will have a wonderful interest in meeting and conversing there with Palamedes, Ajax the son of Telamon, and any other ancient hero who has suffered death through an unjust judgment; and there will be no small pleasure, I think, in comparing my own sufferings with theirs. Above all, I will then be able to continue my search into true and false knowledge—as in this world, so also in the next. And I will find out who is wise, and who pretends to be wise and is not. What would a man not give, judges, to be able to examine the leader of the great Trojan expedition, or Odysseus or Sisyphus, or numerous others, both men and women? What infinite delight would there be in conversing with them and asking them questions! There they do not put a man to death for asking questions—assuredly not. For besides being happier than we are, they will be immortal, if what is said is true.

Therefore, judges, be of good cheer about death, and know for certain that no evil can happen to a good man, either in life or after death. He and his are not neglected by the gods; nor has my own approaching end happened by mere chance. But I see clearly that the time had arrived when it was better for me to die and be released from trouble; therefore the oracle gave no sign. For which reason, also, I am not angry with my condemners or with my accusers; they have done me no harm, although they did not mean to do me any good—and for this I may gently blame them.

Still I have a favor to ask of them. When my sons are grown up, I would ask you, my friends, to punish them. And I would have you trouble them, as I have troubled you, if they seem to care about riches, or anything, more than about virtue; or if they pretend to be something when they are really nothing. Then reprove them, as I have reproved you, for not caring about that for which they ought to care, and thinking that they are something when they are really nothing. And if you do this, both I and my sons will have received justice at your hands.

The hour of departure has arrived, and we go our ways—I to die, and you to live. Which is better, God only knows.

▶ NOTES

1. *agora:* the marketplace in an ancient Greek city [D. C. ABEL, EDITOR]

2. Aristophanes (about 450–388 B.C.E.), who satirized Socrates in his play *The Clouds* [D. C. ABEL]

3. Aristophanes, *The Clouds,* lines 255ff. [B. JOWETT, TRANSLATOR]

4. *natural philosophy:* the philosophy of nature—that is, natural science [D. C. ABEL]

5. Gorgias, Prodicus, and Hippias were Sophists—itinerant teachers who, for a fee, taught Greeks how to succeed in practical affairs. [D. C. ABEL]

6. *political:* pertaining to life as a member of a city-state *(polis)* [D. C. ABEL]

7. *Pythian prophetess:* a priestess of the god Apollo, whose chief oracular shrine was at Delphi [D. C. ABEL]

8. Anaxagoras (about 500–428 B.C.E.) was a Greek philosopher. [D. C. ABEL]

9. The incident from the Trojan War about the son of Thetis (namely, Achilles) that Socrates describes is narrated in Homer's *Iliad,* Book XVIII, lines 94ff. [D. C. ABEL]

10. *gadfly:* a fly that bites cattle [D. C. ABEL]

11. *prytanes:* officials, chosen by lot, who presided over certain activities of the city-state [D. C. ABEL]

12. *deme:* a unit of local government [D. C. ABEL]

13. Homer, *Odyssey,* Book XIX, line 163 [D. C. ABEL]

14. *Prytaneum:* a public hall where the prytanes (see note 11) and other honored citizens, such as victors in the Olympic games, received meals at public expense [D. C. ABEL]

15. *the great king:* the King of Persia, legendary for power and wealth [D. C. ABEL]

# The Republic

Plato

Plato was born in Athens in about 428 B.C.E. As a youth he associated with Socrates, a philosopher who constantly challenged fellow Athenians to think about virtue and to improve their souls. Plato's initial interest was in politics, but he soon became disillusioned, especially when, under the democracy that was restored after the rule of the "Thirty Tyrants," Socrates was arrested on false charges of impiety and the corruption of youth, convicted, and condemned to die. After the execution of Socrates, Plato moved to nearby Megara for a time and may have traveled to Egypt. In 388 he visited Italy and the city of Syracuse in Sicily. Returning to Athens, he founded the Academy, a school devoted both to philosophical inquiry and to the philosophically based education of politicians. Plato spent most of his life teaching at the Academy (Aristotle was his most famous student) and writing philosophical works. He made two more trips to Syracuse, in 368 and 361, apparently with the intention of turning the city's ruler, Dionysius the Younger, into a "philosopher-king." (If this was indeed his purpose, he failed.) Plato died in Athens in 347 at the age of eighty-one.

Most of Plato's works are written as conversations between Socrates and one or more interlocutors on some topic concerning morality. His best-known "dialogues" (the name by which his surviving works are known) are the *Euthyphro, Apology, Crito, Phaedo, Meno, Symposium,* and *Republic.*

Our selection is from the *Republic,* a work cast as a report by Socrates of a conversation he had the previous day with several people, including Glaucon and Adeimantus (Plato's older brothers). In the dialogue Socrates presents his views on a number of topics, but scholars agree these views are Plato's own, not those of the historical Socrates. Our readings are taken from exchanges between Socrates and Glaucon in Books V, VI, and VII.

In Book V Glaucon asks Socrates who the true philosophers are. Socrates, alluding to the etymology of the word ("lovers of wisdom"), says that they are "lovers of the vision of truth." Expanding on this notion, Socrates explains that philosophers are those who love the One rather than the Many. For example, a philosopher goes beyond the love of individual beautiful things to love absolute beauty (beauty itself, the form of beauty). The forms are fully real and are the objects of genuine knowledge, whereas the Many lie between being and not-being and are the objects of mere opinion.

In Book VI Socrates explains that the Many belong to the visible world, which is seen by the eye, while the forms reside in the intelligible world, which is grasped by the mind. He illustrates the two worlds by describing a line divided into two main parts, with each of these parts subdivided into two parts. Each of the resulting four segments of the line represents a type of object of knowledge. Corresponding to each of the four types of object of cognition is a distinct condition in the soul.

Socrates further illustrates this theory of knowledge in Book VII through the famous allegory of the cave. We are like prisoners who live their entire lives inside a cave. Just as such prisoners would think that shadows on the cave wall were real and would be unaware of the real world outside the cave, so we think that the visible world of the Many is real, ignorant of the intelligible world of forms.

▼

Reprinted from *The Dialogues of Plato,* trans. Benjamin Jowett. 3rd ed., vol. 3. New York: Macmillan, 1892.

**Book V**

. . . [Glaucon asked:] Who are the true philosophers?

Those, I [Socrates] replied, who are lovers of the vision of truth.

That is right, he said; but I would like to know what you mean.

I might have difficulty explaining it to someone else, I replied; but I am sure that you will admit a proposition that I am about to make.

What is the proposition?

That since beauty is the opposite of ugliness, they are two.

Certainly.

And inasmuch as they are two, each of them is one.

True again.

And of the just and the unjust, good and evil, and of every other class, the same remark holds; taken singly, each of them is one; but from the various combinations of them with actions and things and with one another, they are seen in all sorts of lights and appear many?

Very true.

And this is the distinction that I draw between the sight-loving, art-loving, practical class of people, and those of whom I am speaking, who are alone worthy of the name of philosophers.

How do you distinguish them? he asked.

The lovers of sounds and sights are, as I conceive, fond of fine tones and colors and shapes and all the artificial products made out of them, but their mind is incapable of seeing or loving absolute beauty.

True, he replied.

Few people are able to attain the sight of this.

Very true.

And he who, having a sense of beautiful things, has no sense of absolute beauty, or who, if another leads him to a knowledge of that beauty, is unable to follow—is such a one awake or in a dream? Reflect: Is not the dreamer, whether asleep or awake, one who likens dissimilar things, putting the copy in the place of the real object?

I would certainly say that such a one was dreaming.

But take the other case, one who recognizes the existence of absolute beauty and is able to distinguish absolute beauty from the objects that participate in it, neither putting the objects in the place of absolute beauty nor absolute beauty in the place of the objects—is he dreaming or is he awake?

He is wide awake.

And may we not say that the mind of the one who knows has knowledge, and that the mind of the other, who opines only, has opinion?

Certainly. . . .

I would ask the person who is of opinion that there is no beautiful in itself or no unchangeable form of beauty itself, but who believes in many beautiful things—the lover of beautiful sights, who cannot bear to be told

© The McGraw–Hill Companies, 2005

that the beautiful is one, that the just is one, or that anything is one—I would ask him this question: Will you be so very kind, sir, as to tell us whether, of all these beautiful things, there is one that will not also appear ugly; or of the just, one that will not also appear unjust; or of the holy, one that will not also appear unholy?

No, he replied; the beautiful will in some way appear ugly; and the same is true of the rest.

And may not the many that are doubles be also halves—that is, doubles of one thing, and halves of another?

Quite true.

And things great and small, heavy and light, as they are termed, will not be denoted by these names any more than by the opposite names?

True; both these and the opposite names will always attach to all of them.

And can any one of those many things that are called by particular names be said to be this rather than not to be this?

He replied: They are like the punning riddles asked at feasts, or the children's puzzle about the eunuch aiming at the bat, with what he hit him, and upon what the bat was sitting.[1] The individual objects of which I am speaking are also a riddle, and have a double sense, and you cannot fix them in your mind either as being or not-being, or both, or neither.

Then what will you do with them? I asked. Can they have a better place than between being and not-being? For they are clearly not in greater darkness or negation than not-being, or more full of light and existence than being.

That is quite true, he said.

We seem, then, to have discovered that the many conventions that the multitude entertain about the beautiful and about all other things are tossing about in some region that is half-way between pure being and pure not-being?

We have.

Yes, and we had agreed earlier that anything of this kind that we might find was to be described as matter of opinion, and not as matter of knowledge—the intermediate flux that is caught and detained by the intermediate faculty.

Quite true.

Then those who see many beautiful things, but who do not see absolute beauty and cannot follow any guide who points the way there; who see many just things, and not absolute justice, and the like—such persons may be said to have opinion but not knowledge.

That is certain.

But those who see the things themselves, which are always the same and unchangeable, may be said to know, and not to have opinion only?

Neither can that be denied.

These persons love and embrace the subjects of knowledge, the others those of opinion? The latter are the same persons, you will remember, who listened to sweet sounds and gazed upon fair colors, but would not tolerate the existence of absolute beauty

Yes, I remember.

Shall we then be guilty of any impropriety in calling them lovers of opinion rather than lovers of wisdom? Will they be very angry at us for describing them in this way?

I shall tell them not to be angry; no man should be angry at what is true.

But those who love the truth in each thing are to be called lovers of wisdom and not lovers of opinion.

Assuredly.

## Book VI

. . . There are many beautiful things and many good things, and so also for other things that we describe and define; to all of them the term "many" is applied.

True, he said.

And there is an absolute beauty and an absolute good, and there is an absolute for all the other things to which the term "many" is applied; for they may be brought under a single form, which is called the essence[2] of each.

Very true.

The many, as we say, are seen but not known, and the forms are known but not seen.

Exactly. . . .

May I suppose that you have this distinction of the visible and intelligible fixed in your mind?

Yes.

Now take a line that has been cut into two unequal parts, and divide each of them again in the same proportion. Suppose that the two main divisions correspond to the visible and to the intelligible. Then compare the subdivisions with respect to their clearness and lack of clearness, and you will find that the first section in the sphere of the visible consists of images. And by images I mean, first shadows, then reflections in water and in solid, smooth, and polished bodies, and everything of that kind. Do you understand?

Yes, I understand.

Imagine now that the other section, of which this is only an image, includes the animals that we see, and everything that grows or is made.

Very good.

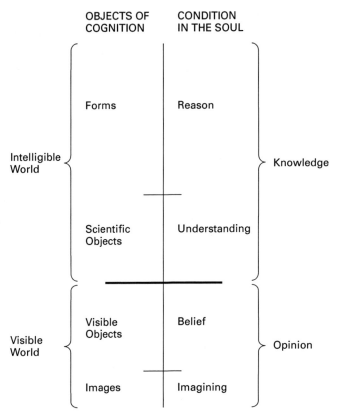

The Divided Line

Would you not admit that both the sections of this division have different degrees of truth, and that the copy is related to the original as the sphere of opinion is related to the sphere of knowledge?

Most undoubtedly.

Next proceed to consider how the sphere of the intelligible is to be divided.

How?

In this way: There are two subdivisions. In the lower one, the soul uses the figures given by the former division as images. This inquiry can only be hypothetical, and instead of going upward to a principle, it descends down to a conclusion. In the higher subdivision, the soul passes out of hypotheses and goes up to a principle that is above hypotheses, making no use of images as in the former case, but proceeding only in and through the forms themselves.

I do not quite understand your meaning, he said.

Then I will try again; you will understand me better when I have made some preliminary remarks. You are aware that students of geometry, arithmetic, and related sciences assume the odd and the even, the various figures, the three kinds of angles, and things related to these in each branch of science. These are their hypotheses, which they and everybody are supposed to know. Therefore they do not think it necessary to give any account of them either to themselves or others; but they begin with them, and go on until they arrive at last, and in a consistent manner, at their conclusion.

Yes, he said, I know.

And do you not also know that, although they make use of the visible forms and reason about them, they are thinking not of these, but of things that they resemble; not of the figures that they draw, but of the absolute square and the absolute diameter, and so on. The things that they draw or make, which have shadows and reflections in water of their own, they use as images; but they are really seeking to see the things themselves, which can be seen only with the eye of the mind.

That is true.

This is the kind of thing I spoke of as intelligible, although in the search for it the soul is compelled to use hypotheses, not ascending to a first principle, because the soul is unable to rise above the region of hypothesis, but employing the objects of which the shadows below are images, and which have a greater distinctness than their images, and therefore have a higher value.

I understand, he said, that you are speaking of the province of geometry and related sciences.

And when I speak of the other division of the intelligible, you will understand me to speak of that other sort of knowledge, which reason itself attains by the power of dialectic,[3] using the hypotheses not as first principles, but only as hypotheses—that is to say, as steps and points of departure into a world that is above hypotheses—in order that it may soar beyond them to the first principle of the whole. Clinging to this first principle and then to that which depends on it, by successive steps reason descends again, without the aid of any sensible[4] object, moving from forms and through forms, and ending in forms.

I understand you, he replied; but not perfectly, for you seem to me to be describing a task that is really tremendous. At any rate, I understand you to say that knowledge and being, which the science of dialectic contemplates, are clearer than the notions of the sciences, as they are called, which proceed from hypotheses only. These notions are contemplated by the understanding, and not by the senses; yet, because they start from hypotheses and do not ascend to a principle, those who contemplate them appear to you not to exercise higher reason upon them, although, when a first principle is added to them, they are intelligible. And I suppose that you would call the mental habit concerned with geometry and related sciences understanding and not reason, because it is intermediate between opinion and reason.

© The McGraw–Hill
Companies, 2005

You have quite sufficiently grasped my meaning, I said; and now, corresponding to these four divisions, let there be four conditions in the soul—reason corresponding to the highest, understanding to the second, belief to the third, and imagining to the last. Let us arrange them in proportion and consider that they have clearness in the same degree that their objects have truth.

I understand, he replied, and give my assent and accept your arrangement.

## Book VII

Next, I said, let me use a comparison to show how far our nature is enlightened or unenlightened. Imagine human beings living in an underground cave that has an entrance open to the light and reaching all along the cave. They have been here since childhood, with their legs and necks chained so that they cannot move and can look forward only, being prevented by the chains from turning their heads. Above and behind them a fire is blazing at a distance, and between the fire and the prisoners there is a roadway. You will see, if you look, a low wall built along the roadway, like the screen that puppeteers have in front of them, over which they show their puppets.

I see.

And do you see, I said, men passing along the wall carrying all sorts of implements, and statues and figures of animals made of wood and stone and various materials, which appear over the wall? Some of them are talking, others silent.

You have shown me a strange image, and they are strange prisoners.

Like ourselves, I replied; and would see they anything of themselves or of one another except the shadows that the fire casts on the opposite wall of the cave?

How could they, he said, if they were never allowed to move their heads?

And of the objects being carried, they would, in like manner, see only the shadows?

Yes, he said.

And if they were able to converse with one another, would they not suppose that they were naming what was actually before them?

Very true.

And suppose further that the prison had an echo that came from the other side. Would they not presume that, when one of those persons carrying the objects spoke, the voice that they heard came from the passing shadow?

No question, he replied.

© The McGraw–Hill Companies, 2005

To them, I said, the truth would be literally nothing but the shadows of the images.

That is certain.

Now look again, and see what will naturally follow if the prisoners are released from their bonds and from their error. At first, when any of them is freed and compelled to stand up suddenly and turn his neck around and walk and look toward the light, he will suffer sharp pains. The glare will distress him, and he will be unable to see the realities of which in his former state he had seen the shadows. And then imagine someone saying to him that what he saw before was an illusion, but that now, when he is approaching nearer to being and his eye is turned toward more real existence, he has a clearer vision. What will be his reply? And you may further imagine that his instructor is pointing to the objects as they pass and requiring him to name them—will he not be perplexed? Will he not consider the shadows that he formerly saw to be truer than the objects now being shown to him?

Far truer.

And if he is compelled to look straight at the light, will he not have a pain in his eyes that will make him turn away to take refuge in the objects of vision that he can see, which he will consider to be in reality clearer than the things now being shown to him?

True, he said.

And suppose that he is reluctantly dragged up a steep and rough ascent, and held fast until he is forced into the presence of the sun itself—is he not likely to be pained and irritated? When he approaches the light, his eyes will be dazzled. And will he be able to see anything at all of what are now called realities?

No, not immediately, he said.

He will need to grow accustomed to the sight of the upper world. First he will see the shadows best, next the reflections of men and other objects in the water, and then the objects themselves. Then he will gaze upon the light of the moon and the stars and the spangled heaven; and he will see the sky and the stars by night better than the sun or the light of the sun by day.

Certainly.

Finally he will be able to see the sun—not mere reflections of it in the water, but in its own proper place and not in another—and he will contemplate it as it is.

Certainly.

He will then proceed to conclude that this is what gives the season and the years, and is the guardian of everything in the visible world, and in a certain way the cause of all things that he and his companions have been accustomed to see.

Clearly, he said, he would do that next.

© The McGraw–Hill Companies, 2005

And when he remembered his old habitation and the wisdom of the cave and his fellow prisoners, do you not suppose that he would count himself happy because of the change, and pity them?

Certainly he would.

And if they were in the habit of conferring honors among themselves on those who were quickest to observe the passing shadows and to remark which of them went before, and which followed after, and which were together, and who were therefore best able to draw conclusions as to the future—do you think he would care for such honors and glories, or envy those who received them? Would he not say with Homer,

Better to be the poor servant of a poor master,[5]

and to endure anything, rather than think as they do and live as they do?

Yes, he said, I think he would rather suffer anything than entertain these false notions and live in this miserable manner.

Imagine also, I said, this man coming suddenly down into the cave and returning to his old place. Would he not be certain to have his eyes full of darkness?

To be sure, he said.

And if there were a contest, and he had to compete in measuring the shadows with those permanent prisoners while his sight was still weak and before his eyes had become steady (and the time needed to acquire this new habit of sight might be very considerable), would he not appear ridiculous? Men would say that up he went and then came down without his eyes, and that it would be better not even to think of ascending. And if anyone tried to free another and lead him up to the light, would they not kill if they could lay their hands on him?[6]

No question, he said.

This entire allegory, I said, you may now append, dear Glaucon, to what we said before. The prison house is the world of sight, the light of the fire is the sun, and if you interpret the journey upward to be the ascent of the soul into the intelligible world, you will not miss what I hope to convey, since that is what you wanted to hear. Only God knows whether it is true. But, whether true or false, my opinion is that in the world of knowledge the form of the good appears last of all, and is seen only with an effort. When seen, it is also inferred to be the cause of all things beautiful and right, parent of light and of the lord of light in this visible world, and the immediate source of reason and truth in the intelligible world. And he who would act wisely either in public or private life must have his eye fixed on it.

I agree, he said, insofar as I am able to understand you.

Moreover, I said, you must not wonder that those who reached this height are unwilling to descend to human affairs; for their souls are ever hastening to the upper world, where they desire to dwell. And this desire is very natural, if our allegory may be trusted.

Yes, very natural.

And is it surprising that one who, passing from divine contemplations to the evils of human life, would behave inappropriately and in a ridiculous manner—who, while his eyes are blinking and before he has become accustomed to the surrounding darkness, is compelled to fight in courts of law, or in other places, about the images or the shadows of images of justice, and compelled to contend with the conceptions of those who have never yet seen absolute justice?

Anything but surprising, he replied.

Anyone with common sense will remember that bewilderment of the eyes is of two kinds and arises from two causes, either from coming out of the light or from going into the light, and he will believe that this is also true of the soul. When one who remembers this sees anyone whose vision is perplexed and weak, he will not be too ready to laugh; he will first ask whether the soul has come out of the brighter life and is unable to see because it is unaccustomed to the dark, or, having turned from darkness to the day, is dazzled by excess of light. And he will count the former soul happy in its condition and state of being, and he will pity the latter one. And if he has a mind to laugh at the soul that comes from below into the light, there would be more reason to laugh at this than to laugh at a soul that has returned from the light above into the cave.

That, he said, is a very just distinction.

But then, if I am right, certain professional educators must be wrong when they say that they can put knowledge into the soul that lacks it, as if putting sight into blind eyes.

They undoubtedly say this, he replied.

But our argument shows that the power and capacity of learning exists in the soul already; and that just as the eye was unable to turn from darkness to light without the whole body, so too the instrument of knowledge can only by the movement of the whole soul be turned from the world of becoming into that of being, and learn by degrees to endure the sight of being, and of the brightest and best of being—namely, the good.

Very true.

---

► NOTES

1.  The children's puzzle illustrates Socrates' point about the same thing having opposite qualities: A eunuch is a man and not a man, a bat is a bird and not a bird, the pumice stone thrown by the eunuch is a stone and not a stone, and the reed the bat was sitting on is a branch and not a branch. [D. C. ABEL, EDITOR]

2.  *essence:* the "what it is" of a thing; its being [D. C. ABEL]

3. *dialectic:* a process of question-and-answer in which one person, by asking a series of probing questions on a topic, stimulates the other person to reflect more deeply on the topic and understand it more fully [D. C. ABEL]

4. *sensible:* able to be sensed [D. C. ABEL]

5. Homer, *Odyssey,* Book XI, lines 489–490. The words are spoken by the ghost of Achilles, the greatest Greek warrior of the Trojan War. Homer (ninth or eighth century B.C.E.) was a Greek epic poet. [D. C. ABEL]

6. Plato alludes to the death of Socrates, whom the Athenians convicted of corrupting the youth and executed. [D. C. ABEL]

# Meno

Plato

Plato was born in Athens in about 428 B.C.E. As a youth he associated with Socrates, a philosopher who constantly challenged fellow Athenians to think about virtue and to improve their souls. Plato's initial interest was in politics, but he soon became disillusioned, especially when, under the democracy that was restored after the rule of the "Thirty Tyrants," Socrates was arrested on false charges of impiety and the corruption of youth, convicted, and condemned to die. After the execution of Socrates, Plato moved to nearby Megara for a time and may have traveled to Egypt. In 388 he visited Italy and the city of Syracuse in Sicily. Returning to Athens, he founded the Academy, a school devoted both to philosophical inquiry and to the philosophically based education of politicians. Plato spent most of his life teaching at the Academy (Aristotle was his most famous student) and writing philosophical works. He made two more trips to Syracuse, in 368 and 361, apparently with the intention of turning the city's ruler, Dionysius the Younger, into a "philosopher-king." (If this was indeed his purpose, he failed.) Plato died in Athens in 347 at the age of eighty-one.

Most of Plato's works are written as conversations between Socrates and one or more interlocutors on some topic concerning morality. His best-known "dialogues" (the name by which his surviving works are known) are the *Euthyphro, Apology, Crito, Phaedo, Meno, Symposium,* and *Republic.*

Our reading is a selection from the *Meno,* a dialogue that addresses the question of how we acquire virtue. Meno, a wealthy young man from Thessaly, asks Socrates how virtue is acquired—by teaching, by practice, or in some other way. Socrates tells Meno he cannot answer any questions about the *qualities* of virtue (what *sort of* a thing it is) because he does not yet know the *nature* of virtue (*what* it is). He then invites Meno to join him in an inquiry into the nature of virtue. Meno responds by trying to force Socrates into a dilemma: If he doesn't know what he is looking for (the nature of virtue), then how can he look for it, or know when he has found it? And if he *does* know what he is looking for, there is no point in searching for it. Socrates thinks this is a false dilemma, and to show why, he recounts to Meno what he heard "from certain wise men and women who spoke of things divine." These wise persons said that the human soul lives on after death, and is reincarnated many times. Before it reenters the world, the soul has knowledge of all that is. After being reincarnated, we do learn, but this learning is really *recollection*—a process of remembering what we knew clearly before we were reborn. Meno's dilemma is false because in a sense we *do* know what we are looking for (we knew it before rebirth), and in a sense we do *not* know, because we have not yet recollected what we previously knew. To demonstrate to Meno that knowledge is recollection, Socrates asks to speak to his slave-boy. By a series of questions, Socrates leads this uneducated boy to remember something that he was unaware of knowing: what geometrical figure has an area exactly twice that of a given square.

*The Dialogues of Plato,* trans. Benjamin Jowett. 3rd ed. vol. 2. New York: Macmillan, 1892 (updated stylistically).

© The McGraw–Hill Companies, 2001

*Meno.* Can you tell me, Socrates, whether virtue is acquired by teaching or by practice? Or, if neither by teaching nor by practice, then whether it comes to man by nature or in [some] other way?

*Socrates.* Meno, there was a time when the Thessalians were famous among the other Hellenes only for their riches and their riding. But now, if I am not mistaken, they are equally famous for their wisdom, especially at Larisa, which is the native city of your friend Aristippus. And this is Gorgias'[1] doing. For when he came there, the flower of the Aleuadae—among them your admirer Aristippus—and the other chiefs of the Thessalians fell in love with his wisdom. And he has taught you the habit of answering questions in a grand and bold style, which [benefits] those who know, and is the style in which he himself answers all comers. And any Hellene who likes may ask him anything. How different is our lot, my dear Meno! Here at Athens there is a dearth of the commodity, and all wisdom seems to have emigrated from us to you. I am certain that if you were to ask any Athenian whether virtue was natural or acquired, he would laugh in your face, and say: "Stranger, you have far too good an opinion of me, if you think that I can answer your question. For I literally do not know what virtue is, and much less whether it is acquired by teaching or not." And I myself, Meno, living as I do in this region of poverty, am as poor as the rest of the world. And I confess with shame that I know literally nothing about virtue—and when I do not know the [nature] of anything, how can I know [its qualities]? How, if I knew nothing at all of Meno, could I tell if he was fair or the opposite of fair, rich and noble or the reverse of rich and noble? Do you think that I could?

*Men.* No, indeed. But are you in earnest, Socrates, in saying that you do not know what virtue is? And am I to carry back this report of you to Thessaly?

*Soc.* Not only that, my dear boy, but you may say further that I have never known of anyone else who did, in my judgment.

*Men.* Then you have never met Gorgias when he was at Athens?

*Soc.* Yes, I have.

*Men.* And did you not think that he knew? . . .

*Soc.* What, according to you and your friend Gorgias, is the definition of virtue?

*Men.* Socrates, I used to be told, before I knew you, that you were always doubting yourself and making others doubt. And now you are casting your spells over me, and I am simply getting bewitched and enchanted, and am at my wits' end. And if I may venture to make a jest upon you, you seem to me both in your appearance and in your power over others to be very like the flat torpedo fish, who [numbs] those who come near him and touch him, as you have now [numbed] me, I think. For my soul and my tongue are really torpid, and I do not know how to answer you. And though I have been delivered of an infinite variety of speeches about virtue before now, and to many persons—and very good ones they were, as I thought—at this moment I cannot even say what virtue is. And I think that you are very wise in not voyaging and going away from home, for if you did in other places as you do in Athens, you would be cast into prison as a magician.

*Soc.* You are a rogue, Meno, and had all but caught me.

*Men.* What do you mean, Socrates?

*Soc.* I can tell why you made a simile about me.

*Men.* Why?

*Soc.* In order that I might make another simile about you. For I know that all [handsome] young gentlemen like to have [handsome] similes made about them—as well they may—but I shall not return the compliment. As to my being a torpedo, if the torpedo is torpid as well as the cause of torpidity in others, then indeed I am a torpedo, but not otherwise. For I perplex others not because I am clear, but because I am utterly perplexed myself. And now I know not what virtue is, and you seem to be in the same case, although you did once perhaps know before you touched me. However, I have no objection to join with you in the inquiry.

*Men.* And how will you inquire, Socrates, into that which you do not know? What will you put forth as the subject of inquiry? And if you find what you want, how will you ever know that this is the thing which you did not know?

*Soc.* I know, Meno, what you mean. But just see what a tiresome dispute you are introducing. You argue that a man cannot inquire either about that which he knows, or about that which he does not know. For if he knows, he has no need to inquire; and if not, he cannot, for he does not know the very subject about which he is to inquire.

*Men.* Well, Socrates, and is not the argument sound?

*Soc.* I think not.

*Men.* Why not?

*Soc.* I will tell you why: I have heard from certain wise men and women who spoke of things divine that—

*Men.* What did they say?

*Soc.* They spoke of a glorious truth, as I conceive.

*Men.* What was it? And who were they?

*Soc.* Some of them were priests and priestesses, who had studied how they might be able to give [an account] of their profession. There have been poets also who spoke of these things by inspiration, like Pindar[2] and many others who were inspired. And they say—mark, now, and see whether their words are true—they say that the soul of man is immortal, and at one time has an end, which is termed dying, and at another time is born again, but is never destroyed. And the moral is that a man ought to live always in perfect holiness.

For in the ninth year Persephone[3] sends the souls of those from whom she has received the penalty of ancient crime back again from beneath into the light of the sun above, and these are they who become noble kings and mighty men and great in wisdom and are called saintly heroes in [later] ages.[4]

The soul then, as being immortal, and having been born again many times and having seen all things that exist, whether in this world or in the world below, has knowledge of them all. And it is no wonder that it should be able to call to remembrance all that it ever knew about virtue, and about everything. For as all nature is akin and the soul has learned all things, there is no difficulty in its eliciting (or, as men say, *learning*) out of a single recollection all the rest, if a man is strenuous and does not faint. For all inquiry and all learning is but recollection. And therefore we ought not to listen to this sophistical argument about the impossibility of inquiry, for it will make us idle, and is sweet only to the sluggard. But the other saying will make us active and inquisitive. Confiding in that, I will gladly inquire with you into the nature of virtue.

*Men.* Yes, Socrates. But what do you mean by saying that we do not learn, and that what we call learning is only a process of recollection? Can you teach me how this is?

*Soc.* I told you, Meno, just now that you were a rogue. And now you ask whether I can teach you, when I am saying that there is no teaching, but only recollection—and thus you imagine that you will involve me in a contradiction.

*Men.* Indeed, Socrates, I protest that I had no such intention. I only asked the question from habit. But if you can prove to me that what you say is true, I wish that you would.

*Soc.* It will be no easy matter, but I will try to please you to the utmost of my power. Suppose that you call one of your numerous attendants, that I may demonstrate on him.

*Men.* Certainly. Come hither, boy.

*Soc.* He is Greek, and speaks Greek, does he not?

*Men.* Yes, indeed; he was born in the house.

*Soc.* Attend now to the questions which I ask him, and observe whether he learns from me or only remembers.

*Men.* I will.

*Soc.* Tell me, boy, do you know that a figure like this is a square?[5]

*Boy.* I do.

*Soc.* And you know that a square figure has these four lines equal?

*Boy.* Certainly.

*Soc.* And these lines which I have drawn through the middle of the square[6] are also equal?

*Boy.* Yes.

*Soc.* A square may be of any size?

*Boy.* Certainly.

*Soc.* And if one side of the figure be of two feet, and the other side be of two feet, how much will the whole be? Let me explain: if in one direction the space was of two feet, and in the other direction of one foot, the whole would be of two feet taken once?[7]

*Boy.* Yes.

*Soc.* But since this side is also of two feet, there are twice two feet?

*Boy.* There are.

*Soc.* Then the square is of twice two feet?

*Boy.* Yes.

*Soc.* And how many are twice two feet? Count and tell me.[8]

*Boy.* Four, Socrates.

*Soc.* And might there not be another square twice as large [in area] as this, and having like this the lines equal?

*Boy.* Yes.

*Soc.* And how many [square] feet will that be?

*Boy.* Eight feet.

*Soc.* And now try and tell me the length of the line which forms the side of that double square. [The side of the original square] is two feet. What will [the side of the double-area square] be?

*Boy.* Clearly, Socrates, it will be double.

*Soc.* Do you observe, Meno, that I am not teaching the boy anything, but only asking him questions. And now he fancies that he knows how long a line is necessary in order to produce a figure of eight square feet, does he not?

*Men.* Yes.

*Soc.* And does he really know?

*Men.* Certainly not.

*Soc.* He only guesses that because the square is double, the line is double.

*Men.* True.

*Soc.* Observe him while he recalls the steps in regular order.

*[To the boy:]* Tell me, boy, do you assert that a double area comes from a double line? Remember that I am not speaking of an oblong, but of a figure equal every way, and twice the size of this—that is to say, of eight feet. And I want to know whether you still say that a double square comes from a double line.

*Boy.* Yes.

*Soc.* But does not this line become doubled if we add another such line here?[9]

*Boy.* Certainly.

*Soc.* And four such lines will make a space containing eight feet?

*Boy.* Yes.

*Soc.* Let us [draw] such a figure. Would you not say that this is the figure of eight feet?

*Boy.* Yes.

*Soc.* And are there not these four divisions[10] in the figure, each of which is equal to the figure of four feet?

*Boy.* True.

*Soc.* And is not that four times four?

*Boy.* Certainly.

*Soc.* And four times is not double?

*Boy.* No, indeed.

*Soc.* But how much?

*Boy.* Four times as much.

*Soc.* Therefore the double line, boy, has given an area not twice, but *four* times as much.

*Boy.* True.

*Soc.* Four times four is sixteen, is it not?

*Boy.* Yes.

*Soc.* What line would give you an area of eight feet? This gave one of sixteen feet, did it not?

*Boy.* Yes.

*Soc.* And the space of four feet is made from this half line?

*Boy.* Yes.

*Soc.* Good. And is not an area of eight feet twice the size of this, and half the size of the other?

*Boy.* Certainly.

*Soc.* Such an area, then, will be made out of a line greater than this one, and less than that one?

*Boy.* Yes, I think so.

*Soc.* Very good; I like to hear you say what you think. And now tell me, is not this a line of two feet and that of four?

*Boy.* Yes.

*Soc.* Then the line which forms the side of eight feet ought to be more than this line of two feet, and less than the other of four feet?

*Boy.* It ought.

*Soc.* Try and see if you can tell me how much it will be.

*Boy.* Three feet.

*Soc.* Then if we add a half to this line of two, that will be the line of three. Here are two and there is one; and on the other side, here are two also and there is one: and that makes the figure of which you speak?

*Boy.* Yes.

*Soc.* But if there are three feet this way and three feet that way, the whole space will be three times three feet?

*Boy.* That is evident.

*Soc.* And how much are three times three feet?

*Boy.* Nine.

*Soc.* And how much is the double of four?

*Boy.* Eight.

*Soc.* Then the figure of eight is not made out of a line of three?

*Boy.* No.

*Soc.* But from what line? Tell me exactly—and if you would rather not [calculate it], try and *show* me the line.

*Boy.* Indeed, Socrates, I do not know.

*Soc.* Do you see, Meno, what advances he has made in his power of recollection? He did not know at first, and he does not know now, what is the side of a figure of eight feet. But *then* he thought that he knew, and answered confidently as if he knew, and had no difficulty. Now he has a difficulty, and neither knows nor fancies that he knows.

*Men.* True.

*Soc.* Is he not better off in knowing his ignorance?

*Men.* I think that he is.

*Soc.* If we have made him doubt and given him the torpedo's shock, have we done him any harm?

*Men.* I think not.

*Soc.* We have certainly, as would seem, assisted him in some degree to the discovery of the truth. And now he will wish to remedy his ignorance, but then he would have been ready to tell all the world again and again that the double area should have a double side.

*Men.* True.

*Soc.* But do you suppose that he would ever have inquired into or learned what he fancied that he knew—though he was really ignorant of it—until he had fallen into perplexity, [realizing] that he did not know and [then feeling a desire] to know?

*Men.* I think not, Socrates.

*Soc.* Then he was the better for the torpedo's touch?

*Men.* I think so.

*Soc.* Mark now the farther development. I shall only ask him, and not teach him—and he shall share the inquiry with me. And do you watch and see if you find me telling or explaining anything to him, instead of eliciting his opinion.

Tell me, boy, is not this a square of four [square] feet which I have drawn?

*Boy.* Yes.

*Soc.* And now I add another square equal to the former one?

*Boy.* Yes.

*Soc.* And a third, which is equal to either of them?

*Boy.* Yes.

*Soc.* Suppose that we fill up the vacant corner?

*Boy.* Very good.

*Soc.* Here, then, there are four equal areas?[11]

*Boy.* Yes.

© The McGraw–Hill
Companies, 2001

*Soc.* And how many times larger is this area than [the original area]?

*Boy.* Four times.

*Soc.* But it ought to have been twice as large only, as you will remember.

*Boy.* True.

*Soc.* And does not this line, reaching from corner to corner, bisect each of these [smaller squares]?[12]

*Boy.* Yes.

*Soc.* And are there not here four equal lines which contain this area?

*Boy.* There are.

*Soc.* Look and see how large this area is.

*Boy.* I do not understand.

*Soc.* Has not each interior line cut off half of the four [smaller squares]?

*Boy.* Yes.

*Soc.* And how many such [halves] are there in this section?[13]

*Boy.* Four.

*Soc.* And how many in this?[14]

*Boy.* Two.

*Soc.* And four is how many times two?

*Boy.* Twice.

*Soc.* And this area is how many [square] feet?

*Boy.* Eight.

*Soc.* And from what line do you get this figure?

*Boy.* From this.

*Soc.* That is, from the line which extends from corner to corner of the figure of four feet?

*Boy.* Yes.

*Soc.* And that is the line which the learned call the "diagonal." And if this is the proper name, then you, Meno's slave, are prepared to affirm that the double area is the square of the diagonal?

*Boy.* Certainly, Socrates.

*Soc.* What do you say of him, Meno? Were not all these answers given out of his own head?

*Men.* Yes, they were all his own.

*Soc.* And yet, as we were just now saying, he did not know?

*Men.* True.

*Soc.* But still he had in him those notions of his—had he not?

*Men.* Yes.

*Soc.* Then he who does not know may still have true notions of that which he does not know?

*Men.* He has.

*Soc.* And at present these notions have just been stirred up in him, as in a dream. But if he were frequently asked the same questions, in different forms, he would know [these things] as well as anyone?

*Men.* I dare say.

© The McGraw–Hill
Companies, 2001

*Soc.* Without anyone teaching him, he will recover his knowledge for himself, if he is only asked questions?

*Men.* Yes.

*Soc.* And this spontaneous recovery of knowledge in him is recollection?

*Men.* True.

*Soc.* And this knowledge which he now has, must he not either have acquired or always possessed?

*Men.* Yes.

---

▶ NOTES

1. Gorgias (about 483–376 B.C.E.) was one of the professional Greek educators known as the Sophists. [D.C.A., ed.]

2. Pindar (about 522–438 B.C.E.) was a Greek lyric poet. [D.C.A.]

3. In Greek mythology, Persephone, with Pluto, ruled over the underworld. [D.C.A.]

4. Pindar, fragment 98 in the Greek edition of August Boeckh; fragment 133 in the Greek edition of Theodor Bergk. [D.C.A.]

5. Socrates here draws a square in the sand. [D.C.A.]

6. Socrates draws a vertical line through the middle (the midpoints) of the top and bottom lines of the square, and a horizontal line through the middle (the midpoints) of the left and right sides of the square. This creates four equal, smaller squares inside the original square. [D.C.A.]

7. *two feet taken once:* that is, two square feet. [D.C.A.]

8. The boy counts the total number of smaller squares drawn inside the larger square. [D.C.A.]

9. Socrates, drawing in the sand, extends one side of the original square to twice its length. [D.C.A.]

10. Socrates has drawn three additional lines, each twice the length of the side of the original square, so that the original square is inside (in a corner of) the new, larger square. He then draws a vertical line connecting the midpoints of the top and bottom sides of the new square, and a horizontal line connecting the midpoints of the left and right sides. This creates in the larger squares four smaller squares, each the size of the original square. [D.C.A.]

11. The resulting figure is one large square composed of four equal, smaller squares. The sides of the smaller squares have a length of two; the sides of the larger square have a length of four. [D.C.A.]

12. Socrates draws a diagonal inside each of the four smaller squares. He draws them so that they form a diamond inside the larger square. [D.C.A.]

13. *this section:* the interior, diamond-shaped square. [D.C.A.]

14. *this:* the original square, from which the larger square was constructed. [D.C.A.]

# On the Soul

Aristotle

Aristotle was born in the town of Stagira in northern Greece in 384 B.C.E. At the age of seventeen, he went to Athens to study at Plato's Academy, where he remained until Plato's death twenty years later. He then spent three years in the city of Assos in Asia Minor and two years in Mytilene on the island of Lesbos. In 343 or 342 he accepted the invitation of King Philip II of Macedon to become the tutor of his thirteen-year-old son, Alexander (later known as Alexander the Great). After a few years at the royal court in Pella, Aristotle returned to Stagira. In 335 he went back to Athens, where he founded a school called the Lyceum. When Alexander died in 323, strong anti-Macedonian sentiment arose in Athens. Because of his connections with Macedon, Aristotle thought it prudent to leave Athens. He went to Chalcis on the island of Euboea, where he died the following year of a stomach ailment.

Aristotle is the author of two very different kinds of philosophical writings: polished works, intended for the general reading public, and notes from which he lectured, intended for circulation among his students and associates. The polished works been have entirely lost except for a few fragments; what has survived is the notes from his lectures on a wide variety of topics including logic, biology, physics, psychology, metaphysics, and ethics.

Our selection is taken from the set of notes called *On the Soul*. In our readings from Book I, Aristotle explains that he will investigate the nature and attributes of the soul, which for him is the principle in a living thing (plant, animal, or human) that makes it alive. He acknowledges the difficulty of the inquiry—especially the difficulty of determining whether any attributes of the soul can exist apart from the body.

In Book II Aristotle defines the soul in terms of "form" and "actuality." All material things are composed of matter ("stuff") and form (that which makes the "stuff" be what it is). In a *living* material thing, the soul, as form, is that which makes the matter (for example, the body of the dog) be the living thing it is (a dog). The soul is also actuality—the principle that makes something that is *potentially* alive (the body of the dog) *actually* alive. The soul, as form or actuality, is the source of all the faculties (capacities) that distinguish living things from nonliving things, such as the faculties of nutrition (common to plants, animals, and human beings), sensation (common to animals and human beings), and thought (uniquely human).

In Book III Aristotle examines the distinctively human capacity of thought. When the mind thinks, it receives the form (essence) of an object and becomes one with it. There is both a passive mind, which receives the forms, and an active mind, which makes these forms present in the passive mind.

▼

**Book I**

**Chapter 1** We regard all knowledge as beautiful and valuable, but one kind more so than another, either in virtue of its accuracy, or because it relates to higher and more wonderful things. On both these counts it is reasonable to regard the inquiry concerning the soul as of the first importance. Moreover, this investigation seems likely to make a substantial contribution to the whole body of truth, and particularly to the study of nature; for the soul is in a sense the principle of animal life. So we seek to examine and investigate first the nature and essence of the soul, and then its [essential] attributes. Of the latter, some seem to be affections[1] peculiar to the soul, and others seem to belong to living things also, by virtue of [their] soul. But to attain any sure belief on the subject is hedged with difficulties on every side. . . .

The affections of the soul present a further difficulty: Are they all shared also by that which contains the soul [namely, the body], or is any of them peculiar to the soul itself? This question must be faced, but its solution is not easy. In most cases, it seems that none of the affections, whether active or passive, can exist apart from the body. This applies to anger, courage, desire, and sensation generally, though possibly thinking is an exception. But if this too is a kind of imagination, or at least is dependent upon imagination, even this cannot exist apart from the body. If then any function or affection of the soul is peculiar to it, it can be separated from the body; but if there is nothing peculiar to the soul, it cannot be separated. In the same way, there are many attributes belonging to the straight qua[2] straight, as, for instance, that a straight line touches a bronze sphere at a point, yet if separated [from the body possessing the attribute of straightness], the straightness will not so touch. It is in fact inseparable, if it is always associated with some body. Probably all the affections of the soul are associated with the body—anger, gentleness, fear, pity, courage and joy, as well as loving and hating; for when they appear, the body is also affected. There is good evidence for this. Sometimes no irritation or fear is expressed, though the provocations are strong and obvious; and conversely, small and obscure causes produce movement when the body is disposed to anger, and when it is in an angry mood. And here is a still more obvious proof. There are times when men show all the symptoms of fear without any cause of fear being present. If this is the case, then clearly the affections of the soul are formulae[3] expressed in matter. Their definitions therefore must be in harmony with this; for instance, anger must be defined as a movement of a body, or of a part or faculty of a body, in a particular state roused by such a cause, with such an end in view. This at once makes it the business of the natural philosopher[4] to inquire into the soul, either generally or at least in this special aspect. But the natural philosopher and the logician will in every case offer different definitions, for example, in answer to the question, What is anger? The latter will call it a craving for retaliation, or something of the sort; the former will describe it as a surging of the blood and heat round the heart. The one is describing the matter, the other the form or formula. . . . For what [the logician] states is the formula of the thing, and if it is to exist, it must appear in appropriate matter. To illustrate this: The formula of a house is a covering to protect from damage by wind, rain, and heat. But another will mean by a house stones, bricks, and timber; and another again will mean the form expressed in these materials to achieve these [ends]. . . .

44

Abel
Discourses

Human Nature

Aristotle
On the Soul (selection)

© McGraw–Hill, Inc., 1995

**Chapter 4** . . . We say that the soul grieves, rejoices, is courageous or afraid, and also grows angry, perceives, and thinks. All these seem to be movements; hence one might suppose that the soul is moved. But this is not a necessary inference. Let us grant that grief, joy, and thinking are all movements—that is, that each of them is a process of being moved; let us further admit that the movement is caused by the soul—for example, that anger and fear are particular movements of the heart, and that thinking is a movement of this or of something else, some of these processes involving change of place and others change of quality in certain parts (of what parts and under what conditions need not be considered now): Still, to say that the soul gets angry, is as if one were to say that the soul weaves or builds a house. Probably it is better not to say that the soul pities, or learns, or thinks, but to say rather that the soul is the instrument whereby man does these things; that is to say, that the movement does not take place in the soul, but sometimes penetrates to it, and sometimes starts from it. For instance, perception starts from particular objects and reaches the soul; recollection starts from the soul and extends to the movements or resting points in the sense organs.

But mind seems to be an independent substance engendered in us, and to be imperishable. If it could be destroyed, the most probable cause would be the feebleness of old age, but, in fact, probably the same thing occurs as in the sense organs; for if an old man could acquire the right kind of eye, he would see as a young man sees. Hence old age is due to an affection, not of the soul, but only of that in which the soul resides, as in the case in drunkenness and disease. Thus the power of thought and speculation decays because something else within perishes, but itself it is unaffected. Thinking, loving, and hating are affections not of the mind, but rather of the individual which possesses the mind, in so far as it does so. Memory and love fail when this perishes; for they were never part of the mind, but of the whole entity which has perished. Presumably the mind is something more divine, and is unaffected. . . .

**Book II**

**Chapter 1** . . . Let us . . . try to determine what the soul is, and what definition of it will be most comprehensive. We describe one class of existing things as substance, and this we subdivide into three: (1) matter, which in itself is not an individual thing; (2) shape or form, in virtue of which individuality is directly attributed, and (3) the compound of the two. Matter is potentiality, while form is realization or actuality, and the word "actuality" is used in two senses, illustrated by the possession of knowledge and the exercise of it.[5] Bodies seem to be pre-eminently substances, and most particularly those which are of natural origin; for these are the sources from which the rest are derived. But of natural bodies some have life and some have not; by life we mean the capacity for self-sustenance, growth, and

Abel
Discourses

Human Nature

Aristotle
On the Soul (selection)

© McGraw–Hill, Inc., 1995

45

decay. Every natural body, then, which possesses life must be substance, and substance of the compound type. But since it is a body of a definite kind—namely, having life—the body cannot be soul, for the body is not something predicated of a subject, but rather is itself to be regarded as a subject, that is, as matter. So the soul must be substance in the sense of being the form of a natural body which potentially has life. And substance in this sense is actuality. The soul, then, is the actuality of the kind of body we have described. But actuality has two senses, analogous to the possession of knowledge and the exercise of it. Clearly actuality in our present sense is analogous to the possession of knowledge; for both sleep and waking depend upon the presence of soul, and waking is analogous to the exercise of knowledge, sleep to its possession but not its exercise. Now in one and the same person the possession of knowledge comes first. The soul may therefore be defined as the first actuality of a natural body potentially possessing life; and such will be any body which possesses organs. (The parts of plants are organs too, though very simple ones. For example, the leaf protects the pericarp, and the pericarp protects the seed; the roots are analogous to the mouth, for both these absorb food.) If, then, one is to find a definition which will apply to every soul, it will be "the first actuality of a natural body possessed of organs." So one need no more ask whether body and soul are one than whether the wax and the impression it receives are one, or in general whether the matter of each thing is the same as that of which it is the matter; for admitting that the terms "unity" and "being" are used in many senses, the paramount sense is that of actuality.

We have, then, given a general definition of what the soul is: It is substance in the sense of formula—that is, the essence of such-and-such a body. Suppose that an implement, for example an axe, were a natural body; the substance of the axe would be that which makes it an axe, and this would be its soul; suppose this removed, and it would no longer be an axe, except equivocally. As it is, it remains an axe, because it is not of this kind of body that the soul is the essence or formula, but only of a certain kind of natural body which has in itself a principle of movement and rest. We must, however, investigate our definition in relation to the parts of the body. If the eye were a living creature, its soul would be its vision; for this is the substance in the sense of formula of the eye. But the eye is the matter of vision, and if vision fails there is no eye, except in an equivocal sense, as for instance a stone or painted eye. Now we must apply what we have found true of the part to the whole living body. For the same relation must hold good of the whole of sensation to the whole sentient body qua sentient, as obtains between their respective parts. That which has the capacity to live is not the body which has lost its soul, but that which possesses its soul; so seed and fruit are potentially bodies of this kind. The waking state is actuality in the same sense as the cutting of the axe or the seeing of the eye, while the soul is actuality in the same sense as the faculty of the eye for seeing, or of the implement for doing its work. The body is that which exists

Abel
Discourses

Human Nature

Aristotle
On the Soul (selection)

© McGraw–Hill, Inc., 1995

potentially; but just as the pupil and the faculty of seeing make an eye, so in the other case the soul and body make a living creature. It is quite clear, then, that neither the soul nor certain parts of it, if it has parts, can be separated from the body; for in some cases the actuality belongs to the parts themselves.

[However,] there is nothing to prevent some parts being separated, because they are not actualities of any body. . . .

**Chapter 2** . . . We say then, assuming a fresh starting-point for our inquiry, that that which has soul is distinguished from that which has not by living. But the word "living" is used in many senses, and we say that a thing lives if any one of the following is present in it: mind, sensation, movement or rest in space, besides the movement implied in nutrition and decay or growth. Consequently all plants are considered to live, for they evidently have in themselves a capacity and first principle by means of which they exhibit both growth and decay in opposite directions; for they do not grow up and not down, but equally in both directions, and in every direction, and they are nourished and continue to live as long as they are able to absorb food. This capacity to absorb food may exist apart from all other powers, but the others cannot exist apart from this in mortal beings. This is evident in the case of plants; for they have no other capacity of the soul.

This, then, is the principle through which all living things have life, but the first characteristic of an animal is sensation; for even those which do not move or change their place, but have sensation, we call living creatures, and do not merely say that they live. The first essential factor of sensation, which we all share, is a sense of touch. Just as the merely nutritive faculty may exist apart from touch and from all sensation, so touch may exist apart from all other senses. (By "nutritive faculty" I mean that part of the soul which even the plants share; all animals obviously possess the sense of touch.). . .

The soul is the origin of the characteristics we have mentioned, and is defined by them—that is, by the faculties of nutrition, sensation, thought, and movement. The further questions, whether each of these faculties is a soul, or part of a soul, and, if a part, whether a part in the sense that it is only separable in thought or also in space, are in some cases easy of solution; but others involve difficulty. For just as in the case of plants some parts clearly live when divided and separated from each other, so that the soul in them appears to be one in actuality in each whole plant, but potentially more than one, so we can see that in other varieties of the soul the same thing happens, for example, in insects which are divided. For each of the parts has sensation and movement in space, and if it has sensation, it must also have imagination and appetite; for, where sensation is, there is also pain and pleasure, and where these are there must also be desire. But in the case of the mind and the thinking faculty, nothing is yet clear; it seems to be a distinct kind of soul, and it alone admits of being separated, as the immortal from the perishable. But it is quite clear from what we have said that the other parts of the soul are not separable, as some say; though it is obvious that they are theoretically different, for there is a difference between the abstract faculties of sensation and opinion, just as feeling is different from opining. The same is true of all the other faculties we have mentioned. Again, some animals have all these faculties, some only some of them, and others again only one. It is this which constitutes the differences between animals. . . .

The phrase "that whereby we live and perceive" has two senses, as has "that whereby we know" (in the one sense we mean knowledge and in the other the soul; for we can say that we know by each of these); similarly, we are healthy either by health or by part or the whole of the body. Now of these, knowledge and health are a kind of shape or form, or notion[6]—an actuality, as it were, of the recipient, that is, of that which is capable of knowledge or health (for the actualization of active processes appears to reside in the patient upon which the effect is produced). And the soul is that whereby we live and perceive and think in the primary sense; so that the soul would be the notion or form, and not the matter or substrate. As we have already said, substance is used in three senses: form, matter, and a compound of the two. Of these, matter is potentiality, and form actuality; and since the compound is an animate thing, the body cannot be the actuality of a soul, but the soul is the actuality of some body. For this reason those are right in their view who maintain that the soul cannot exist without the body, but is not itself in any sense a body. It is not a body; it is associated with a body, and therefore resides in a body, and in a body of a particular kind. . . . From all this it is clear that the soul is a kind of actuality or notion of that which has the capacity of having a soul. . . .

**Book III**

**Chapter 4** Concerning that part of the soul (whether it is separable in extended space, or only in thought) with which the soul knows and thinks, we have to consider what is its distinguishing characteristic, and how thinking comes about. If it is analogous to perceiving, it must be either a process in which the soul is acted upon by what is thinkable, or something else of a similar kind. This part, then, must (although impassive) be receptive of the form of an object—that is, must be potentially the same as its object, although not identical with it: As the sensitive is to the sensible,[7] so must mind be to the thinkable. It is necessary then that mind, since it thinks all things, should be uncontaminated, as Anaxagoras[8] says, in order that it may be in control, that is, that it may know; for the intrusion of anything foreign hinders and obstructs it. Hence the mind, too, can have no characteristic except its capacity to receive. That part of the soul, then, which we call mind (by "mind" I mean that part by which the soul thinks and forms judgements) has no actual existence until it thinks. So it is unreasonable to suppose that it is mixed with the body. For in that case it would become somehow qualitative, for example, hot or cold, or would even have some organ, as the sensitive faculty has—but in fact it has none. It has been well said[9] that the soul is the place of forms,[10] except that this does not apply to the soul as a whole, but only in its thinking capacity, and the forms occupy it not actually but only potentially. But that the perceptive and thinking faculties are not alike in their impassivity is obvious if we consider the sense organs and sensation. For the sense loses sensation under the stimulus of a too violent sensible object; for example, of sound immediately after loud sounds, and neither seeing nor smelling is possible just after strong colours and scents. But when mind thinks the highly intelligible, it is not less able to think of slighter things, but even more able; for the faculty of sense is not apart from the body, whereas the mind is separable. But when the mind has become the several groups of its objects,[11] as the learned man when active[12] is said to do (and this happens when he can exercise his function by himself), even then the mind is in a sense potential, though not quite in the same way as before it learned and discovered; moreover the mind is then capable of thinking itself.

Since magnitude[13] is not the same as the essence of magnitude, nor water the same as the essence of water (and so too in many other cases, but not in all, because in some cases there is no difference), we judge flesh and the essence of flesh either by different faculties, or by the same faculty in different relations; for flesh cannot exist without its matter, but, like "snub-nosed," implies a definite form in a definite matter. Now it is by the sensitive faculty that we judge hot and cold, and all qualities whose due proportion constitutes flesh; but it is by a different [faculty], either quite distinct, or related to it in the same way as a bent line to itself when pulled out straight, that we judge the essence of flesh. Again, among abstract objects, "straight" is like "snub-nosed," for it is always combined with extension; but its essence (if "straight" and "straightness" are not the same) is something different—let us call it duality. Therefore we judge it by another faculty, or by the same faculty in a different relation. And speaking generally, as objects are separable from their matter, so also are the corresponding faculties of the mind. . . .

**Chapter 5** Since in every class of objects, just as in the whole of nature, there is something which is their matter, that is, which is potentially all the individuals, and something else which is their cause or agent in that it makes them all—the two being related as an art to its material—these distinct elements must be present in the soul also. Mind in the passive sense is such because it becomes all things, but mind has another aspect in that it makes all things. This is a kind of positive state like light; for in a sense light makes potential into actual colours. Mind in this sense is separable, impassive, and unmixed, since it is essentially an activity; for the agent is always superior to the patient, and the originating cause to the matter. Actual knowledge is identical with its object. Potential is prior in time to actual knowledge in the individual, but in general it is not prior in time. Mind does not think intermittently. When isolated, it is its true self and nothing more, and this alone is immortal and everlasting (we do not remember[14] because, while mind in this sense cannot be acted upon, mind in the passive sense is perishable), and without this nothing thinks.

▶ NOTES

1. *affections:* states of being affected [D.C.A., ed.]
2. *qua:* as [D.C.A.]
3. *formulae: logoi* in Greek, which could also be translated here as "notions" or "principles" [D.C.A.]
4. *natural philosopher:* philosopher of nature (literally, in Greek, "physicist") [D.C.A.]
5. When one has acquired a knowledge of something (e.g., mathematics), one has actualized one's potential to possess this knowledge. When one *actually exercises* such knowledge (e.g., when using mathematics to solve a problem), one's knowledge is actualized in a different and stronger sense. [D.C.A.]
6. *notion: logos* in Greek, which could also be translated here as "principle" [D.C.A.]
7. *sensible:* able to be sensed [D.C.A.]
8. Anaxagoras (about 500–428 B.C.E.) was a Greek philosopher. [D.C.A.]
9. The reference is probably to followers of Plato. [D.C.A.]
10. In Aristotle's theory of knowledge, when the mind knows something (e.g., a tree), it receives the form of the thing (e.g., treeness) without the matter. [D.C.A.]
11. According to Aristotle, when the mind receives the form of something (see the previous note), it becomes one with the form. As Aristotle states in Book III, Chapter 5, "Actual knowledge is identical with its object." [D.C.A.]
12. *when active:* when exercising his knowledge (see note 5) [D.C.A.]
13. *magnitude:* that is, a physical thing with magnitude [D.C.A.]
14. Aristotle supplies no direct object for the verb "remember"; commentators disagree on what object is implied. [D.C.A.]

# Summa Theologiae

Thomas Aquinas

Thomas Aquinas was born in Roccasecca, Italy, in about 1224. After receiving his initial education from the Benedictine monks at Monte Cassino, he studied at the University of Naples, where he encountered members of the Dominican order. Attracted to the Dominicans, he joined the order despite opposition from his family. He was trained in philosophy and theology in Paris and in Cologne, Germany, under the Dominican Albert (later known as Albert the Great). After being ordained a priest, Aquinas pursued advanced studies in theology at the University of Paris, receiving his degree in 1256. He taught for a few years at the University of Paris and was then assigned to teach at various Dominican schools in Italy. Aquinas returned to the University of Paris in 1268, but four years later he went back to Italy to establish a new Dominican house of study at the University of Naples. He died in 1274 at Fossanova, Italy, while traveling to Lyons to serve as a papal consultant at the Second Council of Lyons.

Aquinas's major works include the *Summa Contra Gentiles* ("Comprehensive Treatise against the Gentiles"), the *Summa Theologiae* ("Comprehensive Treatise on Theology"), *Disputed Questions* (summaries of debates he conducted on various topics as a professor of theology), and detailed commentaries on the principal works of Aristotle.

Our reading is the second "question" (topic) in the Part 1 of the *Summa Theologiae*, "The Existence of God." This question consists of three "articles" (subdivisions). The first article asks whether the existence of God is self-evident. (If God's existence is self-evident, there would seem to be no need to formulate a proof that God exists.) Aquinas contends that God's existence is self-evident *in itself* but not *to us*. A proposition is self-evident in itself if the subject implies the predicate. Since God *is* existence (as Aquinas argues elsewhere), the term "God" implies "existence" and God's existence is therefore self-evident in itself. But God's existence is not self-evident to us because our limited human minds are incapable of grasping the full meaning of the term "God."

Since God's existence is not self-evident to us, Aquinas proceeds to ask, in the second article, whether the existence of God can be demonstrated (proved). He explains that God's existence can be demonstrated by reasoning from effects that we experience, back to God as their cause. In the third article, Aquinas presents five proofs that God exists, based on five kinds of facts that we experience: (1) The fact that there are things in motion implies that there is a first mover that is not itself in motion—and this first mover is God. (2) The fact that there are series of efficient causes (agents that bring things into existence or impart change) implies that there is a first efficient cause—and this first cause is God. (3) The fact that there are possible beings (beings that can not-be) implies that there must be a necessary being (a being that *cannot* not-be) that is its own source of necessity—and this being is God. (4) The fact that there are beings with different degrees of various perfections (for example, of goodness) implies that there is a being that is the cause of all these perfections—and this being is God. (5) Finally, the fact that natural beings without intelligence act for goals (for example, plants act to grow and reproduce) implies that there is an intelligent being that directs natural beings toward their goals—and this being is God.

Note that Aquinas begins each article by formulating objections against his own view. Then, after setting forth his own position, he responds to the objections he had raised.

The *"Summa Theologica"* of St. Thomas *Aquinas, Part I, QQ. I-XXVI,* trans. Fathers of the English Dominican Province. London, England: R. & T. Washbourne, 1911 (updated stylistically).

► PART 1

### Question 2. The Existence of God

**First Article. Whether the Existence of God Is Self-Evident?**  I proceed in this way to the first article: It seems that the existence of God is self-evident.

*Objection 1.* Those things are said to be self-evident to us the knowledge of which is naturally implanted in us, as we can see in regard to first principles. But Damascene says at the beginning of his book, "The knowledge of God is naturally implanted in all."[1] Therefore the existence of God is self-evident.

*Objection 2.* Further, those things are said to be self-evident that are known as soon as the terms are known, which the Philosopher, in the *Posterior Analytics,* says is true of the first principles of demonstration.[2] Thus, when the nature of a whole and of a part is known, it is immediately recognized that every whole is greater than its part. But as soon as the signification of the word "God" is understood, it is immediately seen that God exists. For by this word is signified that thing than which nothing greater can exist. But that which exists actually and mentally is greater than that which exists only mentally. Therefore, because as soon as the word "God" is understood it exists mentally, it also follows that it exists actually.[3] Therefore the proposition that God exists is self-evident.

*Objection 3.* Further, the existence of truth is self-evident. For whoever denies the existence of truth concedes that truth does exist: If truth does not exist, then the proposition "Truth does not exist" is true. But if there is anything true, there must be truth. God is Truth itself: "I am the way, the truth, and the life."[4] Therefore the proposition that God exists is self-evident.

*On the contrary:* No one can mentally admit the opposite of what is self-evident, as is clear from what the Philosopher says in the *Metaphysics* and the *Posterior Analytics* concerning the first principles of demonstration.[5] But the opposite of the proposition "God is" can be mentally admitted: "The fool has said in his heart, 'There is no God.'"[6] Therefore it is not self-evident that God exists.

*I answer:* A thing can be self-evident in either of two ways: on the one hand, self-evident in itself, though not to us; on the other, self-evident in itself *and* to us. A proposition is self-evident because the predicate is included in the notion of the subject, as in "Human beings are animals"—for animal is contained in the formal idea of human being. If, therefore, the essence of the predicate and subject are known to all, the proposition will be self-evident to all—as is clear with regard to the first principles of demonstration, the terms of which are common things that no one is ignorant of, such as being and non-being, whole and part, and so on. If there are some to whom the essence of the predicate and subject are unknown, the proposition will be self-evident in itself, but not to those who do not know the meaning of the predicate and subject of the proposition. Therefore it happens, as Boethius says, that there are some mental concepts self-evident only to the learned, for example, "Incorporeal substances do not exist in space."[7] Therefore, I say that the proposition "God exists" is self-evident itself: The predicate is the same as the subject, because God is his own existence. But since we do not know the essence of God, the proposition is not self-evident to us. but needs to be proved by things that are more evident to us, although less evident in their nature—namely, by effects.

*Reply to Objection 1.* To know that God exists in a general and indefinite way is implanted in us by nature, since God is the beatitude of human beings. For human beings naturally desire happiness, and what is naturally desired by human beings must be naturally known to them. This, however, is not to know absolutely that God exists, just as to know that *someone* is approaching is not the same as to know that *Peter* is approaching, even though it is Peter who is approaching. For many there are who imagine that a human being's perfect good (which is happiness) consists in riches, and others in pleasures, and others in something else.

*Reply to Objection 2.* Perhaps not everyone who hears of this word "God" understands it to signify something than which nothing better can be imagined, seeing that some have believed God to be a material being. Yet, granted that everyone understands that the word "God" signifies something than which nothing greater can be imagined, nevertheless, it does not follow that he understands that what the word signifies exists *actually*, but only that it exists *mentally*. Nor can it be argued logically that it actually exists, unless it be admitted that there exists something than which nothing greater can be imagined; and this precisely is not admitted by those who hold that God does not exist.

*Reply to Objection 3.* The existence of truth in a general way is self-evident, but the existence of a First Truth is not self-evident to us.

### Second Article. Whether It Can Be Demonstrated That God Exists?

I proceed in this way to the second article: It seems that the existence of God cannot be demonstrated.

*Objection 1.* It is an article of faith that God exists. But what is of faith cannot be demonstrated, because a demonstration produces knowledge; whereas faith is of things unseen.[8] Therefore, it cannot be demonstrated that God exists.

*Objection 2.* Further, the essence is the middle term[9] of demonstration. But we cannot know in what God's essence consists, but solely in what it does not consist; as Damascene says.[10] Therefore we cannot demonstrate that God exists.

*Objection 3.* Further, if the existence of God were, demonstrated, this could only be from his effects. But the effects are not proportionate to him, since he is infinite and his effects are finite—and between the finite and infinite there is no proportion. Therefore, since a cause cannot be demonstrated by an effect not proportionate to it, it seems that the existence of God cannot be demonstrated.

*On the contrary,* The Apostle [Paul] says: "The invisible things of God are clearly seen, being understood by the things that are made."[11] But this would not be so if the existence of God could not be demonstrated through the things that are made, since the first thing we must know of anything is whether it exists.

*I answer:* Demonstration can be made in two ways: One is through the *cause* and is called a "demonstration why"; it argues from what is prior absolutely. The other is through the *effect* and is called a "demonstration that"; it argues from what is prior relative to us. When an effect is better known to us than its cause, we proceed from the effect to the knowledge that the cause exists. From every effect the existence of a proportionate cause can be demonstrated, so long as its effects are better known to us. Since every effect depends upon its cause, if the effect exists, the cause must have preexisted. Hence the existence of God, insofar as it is not self-evident to us, can be demonstrated from those of his effects that are known to us.

*Reply to Objection 1.* The existence of God and other similar truths about God that can be known by natural reason, are not articles of faith, but are preambles to them. For faith presupposes natural knowledge, just as grace presupposes nature; and perfection supposes something that can be perfected. Nevertheless there is nothing to prevent someone who cannot grasp its proof from accepting, as a matter of faith, something in itself capable of being known and demonstrated.

*Reply to Objection 2.* When the existence of a cause is demonstrated from an effect, this effect takes the place of the definition of the cause in proof of the cause's existence. This is especially the case in regard to God because, in order to prove the existence of anything, it is necessary to accept as a middle term the meaning of the word and not its essence, for the question of its essence follows on the question of its existence. The names given to God are derived from his effects. Consequently, in demonstrating the existence of God from his effects, we may take for the middle term the meaning of the word "God."

*Reply to Objection 3.* From effects not proportionate to the cause, no perfect knowledge of that cause can be obtained. Yet we can demonstrate the existence of the cause from every effect, and so we can demonstrate the existence of God from his effects, although from these effects we cannot perfectly know God as he is in his own essence.

**Third Article. Whether God Exists?**

I proceed in this way to the third article: It seems that God does not exist.

*Objection 1.* If one of two contraries were infinite, the other would be altogether destroyed. But the word "God" means that he is infinite goodness. If, therefore, God existed, there would be no evil discoverable; but there is evil in the world. Therefore God does not exist.

*Objection 2.* Further, it is superfluous to suppose that what can be accounted for by a few principles has been produced by many. But it seems that everything that appears in the world can be accounted for by other principles, supposing God did not exist. For all natural things can be reduced to one principle, which is nature; and all things that happen intentionally can be reduced to one principle, which is human reason or will. Therefore there is no need to suppose God's existence.

*On the contrary:* It is said in the person of God, "I am who am."[12]

*I answer:* The existence of God can be proved in five ways.

The *first* and more manifest way is the argument from motion. It is certain and evident to our senses that some things are in motion. Whatever is in motion is moved by another, for a thing can be in motion only if it has a potentiality for that towards which it is being moved, while a thing moves insofar as it is actual. For "motion" means the reduction of something from a state of potentiality into a state of actuality.[13] But a thing can be reduced from a state of potentiality into a state of actuality only by something already in a state of actuality. Thus that which is *actually* hot, such as fire, makes wood, which is *potentially* hot, to be actually hot, and thereby moves and changes it. It is impossible for the same thing should be simultaneously in a state of actuality and potentiality from the same point of view, but only from different points of view. What is actually hot cannot simultaneously be only potentially hot; still, it is simultaneously potentially cold. It is therefore impossible that from the same point of view and in the same way anything should be both moved and mover, or that it should move itself. Therefore, whatever is in motion must be put in motion by another. If that by which it is put in motion is itself put in motion, then this also must be put in motion by another, and that by another again. This cannot go on to infinity, because then there would be no first mover, and, consequently, no other movers—since subsequent movers only move insofar as they are put in motion by the first mover, just as the staff only moves because it is put in motion by the hand. Therefore it is necessary to arrive at a first mover, put in motion by no other; and this everyone understands to be God.

The *second* way is from the notion of efficient causation.[14] In the world of things that can be sensed, we find an order of efficient causation. There is no case known (nor is it possible) in which a thing is found to be the efficient cause of itself—for then it would be prior to itself, which is impossible.

In efficient causes it is not possible to go on to infinity, because in all efficient causes following in order, the first is the cause of the intermediate cause, and the intermediate is the cause of the ultimate cause, whether the intermediate cause is several or only one. To take away the cause is to take away the effect. Therefore, if there is no first cause among efficient causes, there will be no ultimate cause, nor any intermediate causes. If it were possible to go on to infinity in efficient causes, there would be no first efficient cause, nor an ultimate effect, nor any intermediate efficient causes—all of which is plainly false. Therefore, it is necessary to posit first efficient cause, to which everyone gives the name of God.

The *third* way is taken from possibility and necessity, and runs as follows. We find in nature things that can either exist or not-exist, since they are found to come to be and then to pass away; consequently, they can exist and not-exist. It is impossible for these [possible beings] always to exist, for that which can not-exist must at one time have not-existed. Therefore, if everything could not-exist, then at one time there would have been nothing in existence. If this were true, even now nothing would exist, because that which does not exist only begins to exist through something that already exists. Therefore, if at one time nothing existed, it would have been impossible for anything to have begun to exist—and thus even now nothing would exist, which is absurd. Therefore not all beings are merely possible beings, but there must exist a being that is *necessary*. But every necessary being either has its necessity caused by another, or not caused by another. It is impossible to go on to infinity in necessary things that their necessity caused by another, as has been already proved in regard to efficient causes. Therefore we must posit a being that is necessary through itself and does it receive its necessity another, and that causes the necessity in other beings. This all men speak of as God.

The *fourth* way is taken from the gradation that is found in things. Among beings, some are more and some are less good, true, noble, and so on. But "more" and "less" are said of different things to the degree that they resemble, in their different ways, something that is the *most;* just as a thing is said to be hotter to the degree that it resembles the hottest. So there is something that is truest, best, and noblest, and consequently being in the highest degree. For things that are true in the highest degree, exist in the highest degree, as stated in the *Metaphysics*.[15] What is most complete in any category is the cause of everything in that category; just as fire, which is the most complete form of heat, causes all hot things, as is stated in the same book.[16] Therefore there must be something that causes the being, the goodness, and every other perfection of all beings; and this we call God.

The *fifth* way is taken from the governance of the world. We see that things lacking intelligence, such as natural bodies, for a goal; this is evident from the fact that they act always, or nearly always, in the same way, so as to obtain the best result. Thus it is plain that they achieve their goal not by accident by but intention. Whatever lacks intelligence can tend toward a goal only if it is directed by some being that has intelligence and knowledge, just as the arrow is directed to its target by the archer. Therefore there is an intelligent being who orders all natural things to their goals,; and this being we call God.

*Reply to Objection 1.* As Augustine says, "Since God is wholly good, he would not allow any evil to exist in his works unless his omnipotence and goodness were such as to bring good even out of evil."[17] It is part of the infinite goodness of God that he allows evil to exist and produces good out of it.

*Reply to Objection 2.* Since nature works out its determinate end under the direction of a higher agent, whatever is done by nature must be traced back to God as to its first cause. Similarly, whatever is done intentionally must also be traced back to some higher cause other than human reason or will. For human reason and will can change and be defective, and things that can change and be defective must be traced back to a first principle that is unchangeable and necessary through itself, as was shown.

▶ NOTES

1. John Damascene, *On the Orthodox Faith* (a Latin translation of *Pēgē Gnōseōs* ["The Fountain of Wisdom"]), Book I, Chapter 1, Section 3. Damascene (about 675–749) was a Greek theologian. [D. C. ABEL, EDITOR]

2. Aristotle, *Posterior Analytics,* Book 1, Chapter 3. Aquinas regularly refers to Greek philosopher Aristotle (384–322 B.C.E.) as simply "the Philosopher." [D.C. ABEL]

3. This argument, now known as the "ontological argument," was first formulated by Italian theologian and philosopher Anselm (about 1033–1109) in his work *Proslogion.* [D.C. ABEL]

4. John 14:6 [D.C. ABEL]

5. Aristotle, *Posterior Analytics,* Book I, Chapter 10; Metaphysics, Book IV, Chapter 3 [D.C. ABEL]

6. Psalms 15:1 (14.1 in some versions); Psalms 53:1 (51:1) [D. C. ABEL]

7. Boethius, *De Hebdomatibus* ("On Groups of Seven," also known as *How Substances Can Be Good in Virtue of Their Existence without Being Absolute Goods*), Point 1. Boethius (about 480–524) was a Roman politician, philosopher, and theologian. [D. C. ABEL]

8. Hebrews 11:1 [D. C. ABEL]

9. *middle term:* in a demonstration, that which connects two elements and allows one to make an inference about the relation of those elements [D. C. ABEL]

10. John Damascene, *On the Orthodox Faith,* Book I, Chapter 4 [D. C. ABEL]

11. Romans 1:20 [D. C. ABEL]

12. Exodus 3:14 [D. C. ABEL]

13. A being has a *potentiality* for receiving a new quality if it can receive it but has not actually done so; it is "reduced" (brought from) potentiality to *actuality* when it receives the new quality. "Motion" here is used in a broad sense that includes not only change in location (locomotion) but other kinds of change as well (such as a qualitative change from cold to hot, to use Aquinas's example). [D. C. ABEL]

14. An efficient cause is an agent that brings a being into existence or brings about a change in a being [D. C. ABEL]

15. Aristotle, *Metaphysics,* Book II, Chapter 1 [D. C. ABEL]

16. Ibid. [D. C. ABEL]

17. Augustine, *Enchiridion,* Chapter 11. Augustine (354–430) was a North African theologian and philosopher. [D. C. ABEL]

# Meditations on First Philosophy

René Descartes

René Descartes was born in La Haye (now called Descartes), France, in 1596. As a youth he was educated by the Jesuits at their college in La Flèche. In about 1614 he began studying at the University of Poitiers, receiving his degree in 1616. Deciding to travel rather than practice law, he went to Holland in 1618 to serve in the army of the Dutch Prince Maurice of Nassau as a gentleman volunteer. One day in November 1619, while on a military tour of Germany, Descartes sat alone in a room reflecting on a new philosophical system that would unify all branches of knowledge and give them the certainty of mathematics. That night he had three dreams, which he interpreted as a divine commission to construct this new system of knowledge. He left the army shortly afterward and traveled for several years. In 1628 he settled in Holland, where he lived for more than twenty years. There he did research in science and in mathematics (laying the foundations for analytic geometry) and developed his philosophy. In 1649, after much hesitation, Descartes acceded to the request of Queen Christina of Sweden to come to Stockholm to tutor her in philosophy. The harsh winter and the rigorous schedule imposed on him by the queen (philosophy lessons at five o'clock in the morning, for example) took their toll on his health: He died of pneumonia in 1650.

Descartes' major works are *Rules for the Direction of the Mind* (written in 1628, published posthumously), *Discourse on Method* (1637), *Meditations on First Philosophy* (1641), *Principles of Philosophy* (1644), and *The Passions of the Soul* (1649).

Our reading is from *Meditations on First Philosophy*. (By "first philosophy" Descartes means truths about the basic topics of philosophy, which for him are God, the soul [mind], and the external world.) In Meditation I, Descartes explains his "method of doubt": He will not accept as true anything of which he cannot be absolutely certain. But practically everything seems open to doubt; Descartes reflects that he might even be deceived in his belief that there is an external world. For how can he be sure that there is not some powerful "evil demon" who tricks him into thinking there is an external world by placing images directly in his mind?

In Meditation II, Descartes realizes that he can be absolutely certain of at least one thing—that he exists, for even if he is deceived about the existence of the external world, he could not be deceived unless he existed. As he formulates this argument elsewhere, "I think, therefore I am." This "I" that exists is "a thing that thinks." Descartes goes on to argue that if there are material things, their essential nature would be extension (three-dimensionality), and that extension is grasped by the mind, not by the senses.

In our selection from Meditation III, Descartes reflects on the certitude of his own existence and formulates a general criterion for truth: "All things that I perceive very clearly and very distinctly are true." He then presents a proof for the existence of God. He finds that his mind contains an idea of an infinite being, and reasons that he himself—who is merely a *finite* being—could not have invented such an idea. Descartes concludes that the idea of an infinite being must have been placed in his mind by the infinite being itself. Therefore this infinite being (God) exists.

▼

Reprinted from *The Philosophical Works of Descartes*, trans. Elizabeth M. Haldane and G. R. T. Ross, Vol. 1. Cambridge, England: Cambridge University Press, 1911 (updated stylistically).

## Meditation I. Of the Things That May Be Doubted

Some years ago I realized how many false beliefs I had from my earliest youth admitted as true, and how doubtful everything was that I had constructed on this basis. From that time I was convinced that I must, once and for all, seriously undertake to rid myself of all the opinions I had previously accepted and start again from the foundation, if I wanted to establish any firm and permanent structure in the sciences. But since this enterprise appeared to be very great, I waited until I had reached an age mature enough so that I could not hope at any later date to be better fitted to carry out my plan. This caused me to delay so long that I feel that I would be wrong to spend in deliberation the time still remaining for me to act. Today, then, since—very opportunely for the plan I have in view—I have freed my mind from every care, and have secured for myself sufficient leisure time in quiet retirement, I will at last seriously and freely address myself to the general destruction of all my former opinions.

Now for this goal it is not necessary for me to show that all of these opinions are false—I could perhaps never be able to do that. But since reason already persuades me that I ought no less carefully to withhold my assent from matters that are not entirely certain and indubitable than from those that appear to me to be obviously false, if I am able to find in each one some reason to doubt, this will be enough to justify rejecting it. And for that goal I will not need to examine each opinion in particular, which would be an endless undertaking. The destruction of the foundations necessarily brings with it the downfall of the rest of the building, so I will only attack those principles upon which all my former opinions rested.

Everything that up to the present time I have accepted as most true and certain, I have learned either from the senses or through the senses. But it is sometimes proved to me that these senses are deceptive, and it is wiser not to trust entirely to anything by which we have once been deceived.

But although the senses sometimes deceive us concerning objects that are hardly perceptible or are far away, there are yet many other things that we cannot reasonably doubt, although we recognize them by means of the senses. For example, there is the fact that I am here, seated by the fire, wearing a dressing gown, holding this piece of paper in my hands, and other similar matters. And how could I deny that these hands and this body are mine—unless I compare myself to certain insane persons, whose brains are so troubled and clouded by the violent vapors of black bile that they constantly assure us that they think they are kings when they are really quite poor, or that they are clothed in purple when they are really without clothing, or who imagine that they have an earthenware head or are nothing but pumpkins or are made of glass. But they are insane, and I would not be any less insane if I took them as a model.

At the same time I must remember that I am a man, and that consequently I am in the habit of sleeping, and that in my dreams I represent to myself the same things or sometimes even less probable ones, than insane persons do in their waking moments. How often has it happened to me that in the night I dreamed that I found myself in this particular place, that I was dressed and seated near the fire, while in reality I was lying undressed in bed! At this moment it does indeed seem to me that I am looking at this piece of paper with my eyes awake, that this head that I move is not asleep, and that I extend my hand deliberately and intentionally and perceive it. What happens in sleep does not appear as clear or distinct as this. But in thinking this over, I remind myself that on many occasions I have in sleep been deceived by similar illusions, and in dwelling carefully on this reflection I see that there are no certain indications by which wakefulness may be clearly distinguished from sleep. I am lost in astonishment, and my astonishment is so great that can almost persuade me that I am now dreaming.

Now let us assume that we are asleep and that all these particulars—for example, that we open our eyes, shake our head, extend our hands, and so on—are false delusions; and let us reflect that possibly neither our hands nor our whole body are what they appear to us to be. At the same time we must at least admit that the things represented to us in sleep are like painted representations that must have been formed as counterparts of something real and true, and that in this way those general things at least (eyes, head, hands, the whole body) are not imaginary things, but things really existing. As a matter of fact even when painters try with the greatest skill to represent sirens and satyrs[1] by strange and extraordinary forms, they cannot give them natures that are entirely new, but merely make a composite of the parts of different animals. Or if their imagination is fertile enough to invent something so novel that nothing similar has ever before been seen, and their work represents a thing that is purely fictitious and absolutely false, it is certain at least that the colors of which the thing is composed are necessarily real. And for the same reason, although these general things—namely, eyes, head, hands, and so on—may be imaginary, we are bound at the same time to admit that there are at least some other objects simpler and more universal, which are real and true. And from these, as from certain real colors, all these images of things that occur in our thoughts (whether true and real or false and imaginary) are formed.

This class of things includes corporeal nature in general and its extension, the shape of extended things, their quantity or magnitude and number, the place in which they are, the time that measures their duration, and so on.

That is possibly why it seems reasonable to conclude from this that physics, astronomy, medicine, and all other sciences that consider composite things, are very doubtful and uncertain; and that arithmetic, geometry, and other sciences of this kind, which deal only with very simple and very general things, without taking great trouble to determine whether they actually exist or not, contain some measure of certainty and an element of the indubitable. For whether I am awake or asleep, two and three together always make five, and a square can never have more than four sides; and it does not seem possible that truths so clear and apparent can be suspected of any falsity.

Nevertheless, I have long had fixed in my mind the belief that an all-powerful God exists, who created me such as I am. But how do I know that he has not brought it about that there is no earth, no heaven, no extended object, no magnitude, no place, and that nevertheless they seem to me to exist just exactly as I now see them? And besides, as I sometimes imagine that others deceive themselves in the things that they think they know best, how do I know that I am not deceived every time that I add two and three, or count the sides of a square, or make judgments about even simpler things, if simpler things can be imagined? But possibly God has not desired that I should be so deceived, for he is said to be supremely good. If, however, it is contrary to his goodness to have made me such that I *constantly* deceive myself, it would also appear to be contrary to his goodness to permit me to be *sometimes* deceived, and nevertheless I cannot doubt that he does permit this.

There may indeed be those who would prefer to deny the existence of a God so powerful, rather than believe that all other things are uncertain. Let us not oppose them for the present, and grant that all that is here said of a God is a fiction. Nevertheless, in whatever way they suppose that I have arrived at the state of being that I have reached—whether they attribute it to fate, to accident, to a continual succession of events, or to something else—since to err and deceive oneself is a defect, it is clear that the less powerful the author to whom they assign my origin, the greater the probability that I am so imperfect as to deceive myself always. To these reasons I have certainly nothing to reply, but at the end I feel forced to admit that there is nothing in all that I formerly believed to be true, of which I cannot in some measure doubt—and this is not through lack of thought or through frivolity, but for reasons that are very powerful and maturely considered. Therefore, in the future I should not less carefully refrain from assenting to these opinions than to what is obviously false, if I desire to arrive at any certainty.

But it is not sufficient to have made these remarks; I must also be careful to keep them in mind. For former and commonly held opinions still return frequently to my mind, since long and familiar custom has given them the right to occupy my mind against my inclination and has rendered them almost masters of my belief. Nor will I ever lose the habit of deferring to them or of placing my confidence in them, so long as I consider them as they really are—that is, opinions in some measure doubtful (as I have just shown), and at the same time highly probable, so that there is much more reason to believe in than to deny them. That is why I think that I will not be acting wrongly if, deliberately taking a contrary belief, I allow myself to be deceived, and for a certain time pretend that all these opinions are entirely false and imaginary, until at last, having in this way balanced my former prejudices with my latter ones, my judgment will no longer be dominated by bad usage or turned away from the right knowledge of the truth. I am assured that there can be neither peril nor error in this course, and that I cannot now yield too much to distrust, since I am not considering the question of action, but only of knowledge.

I will then suppose that not God (who is supremely good and the fountain of truth) but some evil demon, no less powerful than deceitful, has employed his whole energies in deceiving me. I will think that the heavens, the earth, colors, shapes, sound, and all other external things are nothing but the illusions and dreams of which this demon has availed himself in order to lay traps for my credulity. I will consider myself as having no hands, no eyes, no flesh, no blood, no senses, yet falsely believing myself to possess all these things. I will remain obstinately attached to this idea, and if it is not in my power by this means to arrive at the knowledge of any truth, I may at least do what is in my power and, with firm purpose, avoid assenting to any false thing or being imposed upon by this deceiver, however powerful and deceptive he may be. But this task is a toilsome one, and imperceptibly a certain laziness leads me back to the course of my ordinary life. And just as a prisoner enjoys an imaginary liberty while asleep, but fears to awaken when he begins to suspect that his liberty is merely a dream and goes along with these agreeable illusions in order to prolong the deception—so I, imperceptibly of my own accord, fall back into my former opinions and dread awakening from this slumber, lest the waking toil that would follow the tranquility of this slumber would have to be spent not in daylight, but in the excessive darkness of the difficulties that have just been discussed.

### Meditation II. Of the Nature of the Human Mind, and That It Is More Easily Known Than the Body

Yesterday's meditation filled my mind with so many doubts that it is no longer in my power to forget them. And yet I do not see how I can resolve them. Just as if I had suddenly fallen into very deep water, I am so disconcerted that I can neither stand on the bottom, nor swim and bring myself to the surface. I will nevertheless make an effort and follow the same path that I did yesterday—that is, I will proceed by setting aside everything in which the least doubt could be supposed to exist, just as if I had discovered that it was absolutely false. And I will follow this road until I find something that is certain, or at least, if I can do nothing else, until I learn for certain that there is nothing in the world that is certain. Archimedes,[2] in order to shift earth from its place and move it elsewhere, demanded only one fixed and immovable point. In the same way, I will have the right to have high hopes if I am fortunate enough to discover just one thing that is certain and indubitable.

I will suppose, then, that all the things that I see are false; I will persuade myself that nothing has ever existed of all that my fallacious memory represents to me. I will consider that I possess no senses; I will imagine that body, shape, extension, movement, and place are mere fictions of my mind. What, then, can be judged as true? Perhaps nothing at all, except that nothing in the world is certain.

But how can I know there is not something other than those things that I have just considered, which does not allow of the slightest doubt? Is there not some God, or some other being by whatever name we call it, who puts these reflections into my mind? That is not necessary—for is it not possible that I can produce them myself? I myself, am I not at least something? But I have already denied that I have senses and a body. Yet I hesitate, for what follows from that? Am I so dependent on body and senses that I cannot exist without these? But I was persuaded that there was nothing in all the world, that there was no heaven, no earth, that there were no minds, and no bodies. Was I not then likewise persuaded that I did not exist? Not at all; surely I myself did exist, since I persuaded myself of something. But there is some deceiver or other, very powerful and very cunning, who employs his ingenuity in deceiving me. Then without doubt I exist also if he deceives me. And let him deceive me as much as he will, he can never cause me to be nothing so long as I think that I am something. So, after having reflected well and carefully examined all things, I must come to the definite conclusion that the proposition "I am, I exist" is necessarily true each time that I pronounce it, or that I mentally conceive it.

But I do not yet know clearly enough what I am, I who am certain that I am. So I must be careful not to imprudently take some other object to be this "I," and thus go astray in respect to this knowledge that I hold to be the most certain and most evident of all that I have formerly learned. That is why I will now consider anew what I believed myself to be before I began these reflections. I will withdraw all my former opinions that might even in a small degree be invalidated by the reasons that I have just brought forward, in order that nothing at all be left beyond that which is absolutely certain and indubitable.

What then did I formerly believe myself to be? Undoubtedly I believed myself to be a man. But what is a man? Shall I say "a rational animal"? Certainly not; for then I would have to inquire what an animal is, and what rationality is—and thus from a single question I would fall into an infinity of other and more difficult questions; and I do not wish to waste the little

© The McGraw–Hill Companies, 2005

time and leisure remaining to me in trying to unravel subtleties like these. I will instead stop here to consider the thoughts that of themselves spring up in my mind, and that were not inspired by anything beyond my own nature alone when I thought about my being. In the first place, then, I considered myself as having a face, hands, arms, and that whole system of members composed of bones and flesh as seen in a corpse, which I called the body. In addition to this, I considered that I was nourished, that I walked, that I felt, and that I thought; and I referred all these actions to the soul. But I did not stop to consider what the soul was, or if I did stop, I imagined that it was something extremely subtle like a wind or a flame or an ether, spread throughout my more solid parts. As to body, I had no manner of doubt about its nature, but thought I had a very clear knowledge of it. And if I had desired to explain the body according to the notions I had then formed of it, I would have described it as follows: By the body I understand all that can be defined by a certain shape; something that can be confined in a certain place and can fill a given space in such a way that every other body will be excluded from it; something that can be perceived by touch, sight, hearing, taste, or smell; something that can be moved in many ways—not by itself, but by something that is foreign to it, by which it is touched. For to have the power of self-movement, as the power of sensing or thinking, I did not consider to pertain to the nature of body; on the contrary, I was rather astonished to find that faculties similar to them existed in some bodies.

But what am I, now that I suppose that there is a certain demon who is extremely powerful and, if I may say so, malicious, who employs all his powers in deceiving me? Can I affirm that I possess the least of all those things that I have just said pertain to the nature of body? I pause to consider, I revolve all these things in my mind, and I find none of which I can say that it pertains to me. It would be tedious to stop to enumerate them. Let us pass to the attributes of soul and see if there is any one that is in me. What about nutrition or walking? But if I have no body, it is also true that I can neither walk nor take nourishment. Another attribute is sensation. But one cannot have sensation without a body, and besides I have thought I perceived many things during sleep that, in my waking moments, I realized that I did not experience at all. What about thinking? I find here that thought is an attribute that belongs to me; it alone cannot be separated from me. I am, I exist; that is certain. But how often? Just when I think; for it might possibly be the case if I ceased entirely to think, that I would likewise cease entirely to exist. I do not now admit anything that is not necessarily true. To speak accurately, I am no more than a thing that thinks—that is to say, a mind, or soul, or intellect, or reason, which are terms whose significance was formerly unknown to me. I am, however, a real thing and really exist. But what thing? I have answered: a thing that thinks.

And what more? I will exercise my imagination. I am not a collection of members that we call the human body; I am not a subtle air distributed through these members; I am not a wind, a fire, a vapor, a breath, or anything at all that I can imagine or conceive—because I have assumed that all these were nothing. Without changing that supposition, I find myself certain only of the fact that I am something. But perhaps it is true that these same things that I supposed were nonexistent because they are unknown to me, are really not different from the self that I know. I am not sure about this, and I will not dispute about it now; I can only judge things that are known to me. I know that I exist, and I inquire what I am, I whom I know to exist. But it is very certain that the knowledge of my existence taken in its precise significance does not depend on things whose existence is not yet known to me; consequently it does not depend on those that I can invent in imagination. And indeed the very term "invent" proves to me my error, for I really do this if I imagine myself as something, since to imagine is nothing else than to contemplate the shape or image of a corporeal thing. But I already know for certain that I am, and that it may be that all these images, and, speaking generally, all things that relate to the nature of body, are nothing but dreams. For this reason I see clearly that I have as little reason to say, "I will stimulate my imagination in order to know more distinctly what I am," than if I were to say, "I am now awake, and I perceive something that is real and true; but because I do not yet perceive it distinctly enough, I will deliberately go to sleep so that my dreams may represent the perception with the greatest truth and evidence." And thus I know for certain that nothing of all that I can understand by means of my imagination belongs to this knowledge that I have of myself, and that it is necessary to recall the mind from this mode of thought with the utmost diligence in order that it may be able to know its own nature with perfect distinctness.

But what then am I? A thing that thinks. What is a thing that thinks? A thing that doubts, understands, affirms, denies, wills, refuses, and also imagines and has sensations. . . .

[Consider] the things that we most commonly believe to be the most distinctly comprehended, namely, the bodies that we touch and see—not bodies in general, for these general ideas are usually a little more confused, but one body in particular. Let us take, for example, this piece of wax: It has just been taken from the hive, and it has not yet lost the sweetness of the honey it contains; it still retains some of the odor of the flowers from which it has been collected; its color, shape, and size are apparent; it is hard, cold, easily handled; and if you strike it with your knuckle, it will emit a sound. Finally, all the things necessary to cause us to distinctly recognize a body are present in it. But notice that while I speak and approach the fire, what remained of the taste is eliminated, the smell evaporates, the color alters, the shape is destroyed, the size increases, it becomes liquid and hot and one can hardly handle it, and when it is struck, no sound is emitted. Does the same wax remain after this change? We must admit that it remains; no one would judge otherwise. What then did I know so distinctly in this piece of wax? It could certainly be none of the things that the senses brought to my notice, since everything that falls under taste, smell, sight, touch, and hearing, is found to be changed, and yet the same wax remains.

Perhaps it was what I now think, namely, that this wax was not the sweetness of honey, or the agreeable scent of flowers, or the whiteness, or the shape, or the sound, but simply a body that a little while before appeared to me as perceptible under these forms, and that is now perceptible under others. But what, precisely, is it that I imagine when I form such conceptions? Let us attentively consider this, and, taking away all that does not belong to the wax, let us see what remains. Certainly nothing remains except a certain extended thing that is flexible and movable. But what is the meaning of "flexible" and "movable"? Is it not that I imagine that this round piece of wax is able to become square and to pass from a square to a triangular shape? No, certainly it is not that, since I imagine it admits of an infinity of similar changes, and I nevertheless do not know how to encompass this infinity by my imagination, and consequently this conception I have of the wax is not brought about by the faculty of imagination. What now is this extension? Is it not also unknown? For it becomes greater when the wax is melted, greater when it is boiled, and still greater when the heat increases. And I would not conceive rightly what wax is, if I did not think that even this piece that we are considering is capable of receiving more variations in extension than I have ever imagined. We must then grant that I could not even understand through the imagination what this piece of wax is, and that it is my mind alone that perceives it. I am speaking of this piece of wax in particular, but for wax in general it is even clearer. But what is this piece of wax that cannot be understood except by the mind? It is certainly the same wax that I see, touch, imagine; in short, it is the same wax that I have always believed it to be from the beginning. But what must particularly be observed is that its perception is not an act of vision, touch, or imagination (and has never been such, although it may have previously appeared to be so), but only an intuition of the mind, which may be imperfect and confused as it was formerly, or clear and distinct as it is at present, according to the degree of attention I pay to the elements that are found in it, and of which it is composed.

Yet in the meantime I am greatly astonished when I consider the how feeble the mind is and how prone to error. Although I consider all this in my own mind without giving external expression to my thoughts, words often impede me and I am almost deceived by the terms of ordinary language. For we say that we see the same wax, if it is present, and not that we simply judge that it is the same from its having the same color and shape.

From this I might conclude that I knew the wax by means of vision and not simply by the intuition of the mind—unless I happen to remember that, when looking from a window and saying that I see men passing in the street, I really do not see them, but *infer* that what I see is men, just as I say that I see wax. And yet what do I see from the window except hats and coats that may cover automatons? Yet I judge these to be men. And similarly, solely by the faculty of judgment that rests in my mind do I comprehend what I believed I saw with my eyes. . . .

## Meditation III. Of God, That He Exists

I will now close my eyes, stop my ears, and divert all my senses. I will eliminate even from my thoughts all the images of corporeal things, or (since that is hardly possible) at least I will judge them as empty and false. And thus conversing only with myself and considering my own nature, I will try little by little to reach a better knowledge of and acquaintance with myself. I am a thing that thinks—that is, a thing that doubts, affirms, denies, knows a few things and is ignorant of many things, wills, desires, and also imagines and perceives. For, as I remarked before, although the things that I perceive and imagine are perhaps nothing at all apart from me and in themselves, I am nevertheless certain that these modes of thought that I call perceptions and imaginations, insofar as they are only modes of thought, certainly reside in me.

And in the little that I have just said, I think I have summed up all that I really know, or at least all that, so far, I have discovered that I know. In order to try to extend my knowledge further, I will now look around more carefully and see whether I cannot still discover in myself some other things that I have not previously perceived. I am certain that I am a thing that thinks. But do I not then likewise know what is necessary to make me certain of a truth? Certainly in this initial knowledge there is nothing that assures me of its truth, except the clear and distinct perception of what I affirm. And this would not suffice to assure me that what I say is true, if it could ever happen that a thing that I conceived so clearly and distinctly could be false. Accordingly, it seems to me that already I can establish as a general rule that all things that I perceive very clearly and very distinctly are true. . . .

Among my ideas, some appear to me to be innate, some adventitious,[3] and others formed by myself. My power of understanding what a thing is, or a truth is, or a thought is, appears to me to come from any source other than my own nature. But if I now hear some sound, see the sun, or feel heat, I have previously judged that these sensations proceeded from certain things existing outside of me. And finally it seems to me that sirens, hippogriffs,[4] and the like, are formed out of my own mind. But again I may possibly persuade myself that all these ideas are what I call adventitious, or else that they are all innate, or all fictitious—for I have not yet clearly discovered their true origin.

My principal task now is to consider, with respect to those ideas that appear to me to proceed from certain objects outside me, the reasons that cause me to think that these ideas are similar to the objects. It seems indeed, in the first place, that I am taught this lesson by nature; and, secondly, I experience in myself that these ideas do not depend on my will or therefore on myself—for they often present themselves to my mind in spite of my will. Just now, for instance, whether I will it or do not will it, I feel heat; and thus I persuade myself that this feeling or idea of heat is produced in me by something different from me, namely, the heat of the fire near which I sit. And nothing seems to me more obvious than the judgment that this object imprints its likeness rather than anything else upon me.

Now I must discover whether these proofs are sufficiently strong and convincing. When I say that I am taught by nature, I merely mean a certain spontaneous inclination that impels me to believe in this connection, and not a natural light that makes me recognize that it is true. These two things are very different; for I cannot doubt that which the natural light causes me to believe to be true—for example, that it follows from the fact that I doubt, that I exist; or other facts of this same kind. I possess no other faculty that is equally trustworthy for distinguishing truth from falsehood, which could teach me that what this natural light shows me to be true is not really true. But as far as natural impulses are concerned, I have frequently noticed that, when I had to actively choose between virtue and vice, they often enough led me to the worse choice; and this is why I do not see any reason for following them with regard to truth and error.

And as to the other reason—namely, that these ideas must proceed from objects outside me, since they do not depend on my will—I do not find it any more convincing. For just as these impulses of which I have spoken are found in me, even though they do not always concur with my will, so perhaps there is in me some faculty capable of producing these ideas without the assistance of any external things, even though it is not yet known by me—just as they apparently are produced in me during sleep, without the aid of any external objects.

And finally, though they did proceed from objects different from myself, it is not necessary that they should resemble these objects. On the contrary, I have noticed that in many cases there was a great difference between the object and its idea. I find, for example, two completely different ideas of the sun in my mind. One derives from the senses, and should be placed in the category of adventitious ideas; according to this idea, the sun seems to be extremely small. The other derives from astronomical reasoning,—that is, it derives from certain notions innate in me (or else it is formed by me in some other way)—and in accordance with this, the sun appears to be several times greater than the earth. These two ideas cannot, indeed, both resemble the same sun, and reason makes me believe that the one that seems to have originated directly from the sun itself is the one most dissimilar to the sun.

All this causes me to believe that, up until the present time, it has not been by a judgment that was certain but only by a sort of blind impulse that I believed that things exist outside of me and different from me and convey their ideas or images to me by the organs of my senses, or by some other method, whatever it might be. . . .

But among my ideas, in addition to the idea that represents me to myself, concerning which there can here be no difficulty, there is another that represents God, others that represent corporeal and inanimate things, angels, and animals, and others that represent men like myself.

With regard to the ideas that represent other men, or animals, or angels, I can however easily conceive that they might be formed by a mixture of the other ideas that I have of myself, of corporeal things, and of God—even if, apart from me, no men or animals or angels existed in all the world.

With regard to the ideas of corporeal objects, I do not recognize in them anything so great or so excellent that they might not have possibly proceeded from myself. . . .

There remains only the idea of God, concerning which we must consider whether it is something that cannot have proceeded from myself. By the word "God" I understand a substance that is infinite, independent, all-knowing, all-powerful, and that created me and everything else (if there is anything else). All these characteristics are such that the more diligently I attend to them, the less they appear capable of proceeding from me alone. Therefore, from what has been already said, we must conclude that God necessarily exists.

For although the idea of *substance* is in me because of the fact I am substance, nevertheless I would not have the idea of an *infinite* substance—since I am finite—if it had not proceeded from some substance that was truly infinite.

Nor should I imagine that I do not perceive the infinite by a true idea, but only by the negation of the finite, just as I perceive rest and darkness by the negation of movement and light. On the contrary, I see that there is clearly more reality in infinite substance than in finite substance, and therefore that in some way I have in me the notion of the infinite before the notion of the finite—that is to say, the notion of God before that of myself. For how would it be possible for me to know that I doubt and desire (that is, that I lack something) and that I am not wholly perfect, unless I had in me some idea of a being more perfect than myself, in comparison with which I recognize the deficiencies of my nature? . . .

It only remains to me to examine how I have acquired this idea from God. For I have not received it through the senses, and it is never presented to me unexpectedly, as usually happens with ideas of things perceivable by the senses, when these things present themselves (or seem to present themselves) to my external sense organs. Nor is it a fiction of my mind, for it is not in my power to take from it or to add anything to it. Consequently the only alternative is that it is innate in me, just as the idea of myself is innate in me.

---

▶ NOTES

1. In Greek mythology, *sirens* are female and partly human creatures who lure sailors to their destruction with their beautiful singing; *satyrs* are woodland creatures with features of both a horse and a goat, fond of unrestrained revelry. [D. C. ABEL, EDITOR]

2. Archimedes (about 287–212 B.C.E.) was a Greek mathematician and inventor. [D. C. ABEL]

3. *adventitious:* coming from an external source [D. C. ABEL]

4. *hippogriffs:* mythical animals that are part horse and part griffin (a griffin is a mythical animal that is part eagle and part lion) [D. C. ABEL]

# Meditations on First Philosophy

René Descartes

René Descartes was born in La Haye (now called Descartes), France, in 1596. As a youth he was educated by the Jesuits at their college in La Flèche. In about 1614 he began studying at the University of Poitiers, receiving his degree in 1616. Deciding to travel rather than practice law, he went to Holland in 1618 to serve in the army of the Dutch Prince Maurice of Nassau as a gentleman volunteer. One day in November 1619, while on a military tour of Germany, Descartes sat alone in a room reflecting on a new philosophical system that would unify all branches of knowledge and give them the certainty of mathematics. That night he had three dreams, which he interpreted as a divine commission to construct this new system of knowledge. He left the army shortly afterwards and traveled for several years. In 1628 he settled in Holland, where he lived for more than twenty years. There he did research in science and in mathematics (laying the foundations for analytic geometry) and developed his philosophy. In 1649, after much hesitation, Descartes acceded to the request of Queen Christina of Sweden to come to Stockholm to tutor her in philosophy. The harsh winter and the rigorous schedule imposed on him by the queen (philosophy lessons at five o'clock in the morning, for example) took their toll on his health: He died of pneumonia in 1650.

Descartes' major works are *Rules for the Direction of the Mind* (written in 1628, published posthumously), *Discourse on Method* (1637), *Meditations on First Philosophy* (1641), *Principles of Philosophy* (1644), and *The Passions of the Soul* (1649).

Our selection is from *Meditations on First Philosophy*. (By "first philosophy" Descartes means truths about the basic topics of philosophy, which for him are God, the soul [mind], and the external world.) Our reading begins with Meditation II, in which Descartes tries to find something of which he can be absolutely certain—something about which not even a powerful "evil demon" could deceive him. Descartes points out that he might be deceived even about such seemingly obvious things as the existence of the external world. But there is one thing he can be certain of—that he exists. For it would not even be possible for him to be deceived, if he did not exist. As he formulates this argument elsewhere, "I think, therefore I am." But what is this "I" that exists? Descartes argues that since he could be deceived about having a body, he is simply "a thing that thinks." He goes on to point out that if material things do exist, their essential nature would be extension (three-dimensionality).

In Meditation V, Descartes presents a proof for God's existence. Descartes has an idea of a supremely perfect being, and since existence is a necessary attribute of such a being, his idea would be self-contradictory if God did not exist. In the sixth and final meditation, Descartes uses his knowledge that God exists to prove that the external world exists: Since God is good and not a deceiver, it would be contrary to God's nature to give someone the inclination to believe that material things (including one's body) exist, if they didn't actually exist. Descartes has a body, then, but how is he (a thinking, nonextended thing) related to it (an extended, nonthinking thing)? Descartes states (with little further explanation) that he is "very closely united to it and, so to speak . . . intermingled with it."

▼

Reprinted from *The Philosophical Works of Descartes*, trans. Elizabeth M. Haldane and G. R. T. Ross, Vol. 1. Cambridge, England: Cambridge University Press, 1911 (updated stylistically).

### Meditation II. Of the Nature of the Human Mind, and That It Is More Easily Known Than the Body

... I will proceed by setting aside everything in which the least doubt could be supposed to exist, just as if I had discovered that it was absolutely false. And I will follow this road until I find something which is certain, or at least, if I can do nothing else, until I learn for certain that there is nothing in the world that is certain. Archimedes,[1] in order to shift the earth from its place and move it elsewhere, demanded only one fixed and immovable point. In the same way, I will have the right to have high hopes if I am fortunate enough to discover one thing only that certain and indubitable.

I will suppose, then, that all the things that I see are false; I will persuade myself that nothing has ever existed of all that my fallacious memory represents to me. I will consider that I possess no senses; I will imagine that body, shape, extension, movement, and place are mere fictions of my mind. What, then, can be judged as true? Perhaps nothing at all, except that nothing in the world is certain.

But how can I know there is not something other than those things that I have just considered, which does not allow of the slightest doubt? Is there not some God, or some other being by whatever name we call it, who puts these reflections into my mind? That is not necessary—for is it not possible that I can produce them myself? I myself, am I not at least something? But I have already denied that I have senses and body. Yet I hesitate, for what follows from that? Am I so dependent on body and senses that I cannot exist without these? But I was persuaded that there was nothing in all the world, that there was no heaven, no earth, that there were no minds, and no bodies. Was I not then likewise persuaded that I did not exist? Not at all; surely I myself did exist, since I persuaded myself of something. But there is some deceiver or other, very powerful and very cunning, who employs his ingenuity in deceiving me. Then without doubt I exist also if he deceives me. And let him deceive me as much as he will, he can never cause me to be nothing so long as I think that I am something. So, after having reflected well and carefully examined all things, I must come to the definite conclusion that the proposition "I am, I exist" is necessarily true each time that I pronounce it, or that I mentally conceive it.

But I do not yet know clearly enough what I am, I who am certain that I am. So I must be careful not to imprudently take some other object to be this "I," and thus go astray in respect to this knowledge that I hold to be the most certain and most evident of all that I have formerly learned. That is why I will now consider anew what I believed myself to be before I began these reflections. I will withdraw all my former opinions that might even in a small degree be invalidated by the reasons that I have just brought forward, in order that nothing at all be left beyond that which is absolutely certain and indubitable.

What then did I formerly believe myself to be? Undoubtedly I believed myself to be a man. But what is a man? Shall I say "a rational animal"? Certainly not; for then I would have to inquire what an animal is, and what rationality is—and thus from a single question I would fall into an infinity of other and more difficult questions; and I do not wish to waste the little time and leisure remaining to me in trying to unravel subtleties like these. I will instead stop here to consider the thoughts that of themselves spring up in my mind, and that were not inspired by anything beyond my own nature alone when I thought about my being. In the first place, then, I considered myself as having a face, hands, arms, and that whole system of members composed of bones and flesh as seen in a corpse, which I called the body. In addition to this, I considered that I was nourished, that I walked, that I felt, and that I thought; and I referred all these actions to the soul. But I did not stop to consider what the soul was, or if I did stop, I imagined that it was something extremely subtle like a wind or a flame or an ether, spread throughout my more solid parts. As to body, I had no manner of doubt about its nature, but thought I had a very clear knowledge of it. And if I had desired to explain the body according to the notions I had then formed of it, I would have described it as follows: By the body I understand all that can be defined by a certain shape; something that can be confined in a certain place and can fill a given space in such a way that every other body will be excluded from it; something that can be perceived by touch, sight, hearing, taste, or smell; something that can be moved in many ways—not by itself, but by something that is foreign to it, by which it is touched. For to have the power of self-movement, as the power of sensing or thinking, I did not consider to pertain to the nature of body; on the contrary, I was rather astonished to find that faculties similar to them existed in some bodies.

But what am I, now that I suppose that there is a certain demon who is extremely powerful and, if I may say so, malicious, who employs all his powers in deceiving me? Can I affirm that I possess the least of all those things that I have just said pertain to the nature of body? I pause to consider, I revolve all these things in my mind, and I find none of which I can say that it pertains to me. It would be tedious to stop to enumerate them. Let us pass to the attributes of soul and see if there is any one that is in me. What about nutrition or walking? But if I have no body, it is also true that I can neither walk nor take nourishment. Another attribute is sensation. But one cannot have sensation without a body, and besides I have thought I perceived many things during sleep that, in my waking moments, I realized that I did not experience at all. What about thinking? I find here that thought is an attribute that belongs to me; it alone cannot be separated from me. I am, I exist; that is certain. But how often? Just when I think; for it might possibly be the case if I ceased entirely to think, that I would likewise cease entirely to exist. I do not now admit anything that is not necessarily true. To speak accurately, I am no more than a thing that thinks—that is to say, a mind, or soul, or intellect, or reason, which are terms whose significance was formerly unknown to me. I am, however, a real thing and really exist. But what thing? I have answered: a thing that thinks.

And what more? I will exercise my imagination. I am not a collection of members that we call the human body; I am not a subtle air distributed through these members; I am not a wind, a fire, a vapor, a breath, or anything at all that I can imagine or conceive—because I have assumed that all these were nothing. Without changing that supposition, I find myself certain only of the fact that I am something. But perhaps it is true that these same things that I supposed were nonexistent because they are unknown to me, are really not different from the self that I know. I am not sure about this, and I will not dispute about it now; I can only judge things that are known to me. I know that I exist, and I inquire what I am, I whom I know to exist. But it is very certain that the knowledge of my existence taken in its precise significance does not depend on things whose existence is not yet known to me; consequently it does not depend on those that I can invent in imagination. And indeed the very term "invent" proves to me my error, for I really do this if I imagine myself as something, since to imagine is nothing else than to contemplate the shape or image of a corporeal thing. But I already know for certain that I am, and that it may be that all these images, and, speaking generally, all things that relate to the nature of body, are nothing but dreams. For this reason I see clearly that I have as little reason to say, "I will stimulate my imagination in order to know more distinctly what I am," than if I were to say, "I am now awake, and I perceive something that is real and true; but because I do not yet perceive it distinctly enough, I will deliberately go to sleep so that my dreams may represent the perception with the greatest truth and evidence." And thus I know for certain that nothing of all that I can understand by means of my imagination belongs to this knowledge that I have of myself, and that it is necessary to recall the mind from this mode of thought with the utmost diligence in order that it may be able to know its own nature with perfect distinctness.

But what then am I? A thing that thinks. What is a thing that thinks? A thing that doubts, understands, affirms, denies, wills, refuses, and also imagines and has sensations.

Certainly it is no small matter if all these things pertain to my nature. But why should they not pertain to it? Am I not that being who now doubts nearly everything, who nevertheless understands certain things, who affirms that this one thing is true, who denies all the others, who desires to know more, who does not want to be deceived, who imagines many things (sometimes indeed despite his will), and who likewise perceives many things, as if by the senses? Is there nothing in all this that is just as true as that fact that I exist, even if I am always asleep and even if the one who has given me being employs all his ingenuity in deceiving me? Is there any one of these attributes that can be distinguished from my thought, or that might be said to be separate from myself? For it is so evident that it is I who doubt, understand, and desire, that there is no reason here to add anything to explain it. And I have certainly the power of imagining; for although it may happen (as I formerly supposed) that none of the things that I imagine are true, nevertheless this power of imagining does not cease to be real, and it is a part of my thought. Finally, I am the same one who senses, or who perceives certain things as if through the senses, since I see light, hear noise, and feel heat. But it will be said that these phenomena are false and that I am dreaming. Let it be so; still it is at least quite certain that it *seems* to me that I see light, hear noise, and feel heat. That cannot be false; properly speaking, it is what is in me called "sensing," and used in this precise sense of the term it is nothing other than thinking.

From this I am beginning to know what I am a little better than I did before; but nevertheless it still seems to me—and I cannot prevent myself from thinking this—that corporeal things, whose images are formed by thought and which are tested by the senses, are much more distinctly known than that obscure part of me that does not come under the imagination. But it is very strange to say that I know and understand more distinctly things whose existence seems to me doubtful, which are unknown to me, and which do not belong to me, than others which I am convinced are true, which are known to me, and which pertain to my real nature—namely, myself. But I see clearly how the case stands: My mind loves to wander, and cannot yet allow itself to be restrained within the limits of truth. Very well; let us once more give it free rein, so that when we pull in the reins at the proper time, it will more easily be regulated and controlled.

Let us begin by considering the things that we most commonly believe to be the most distinctly comprehended, namely, the bodies that we touch and see—not bodies in general, for these general ideas are usually a little more confused, but one body in particular. Let us take, for example, this piece of wax: It has just been taken from the hive, and it has not yet lost the sweetness of the honey it contains; it still retains some of the odor of the flowers from which it has been collected; its color, shape, and size are apparent; it is hard, cold, easily handled; and if you strike it with your knuckle, it will emit a sound. Finally, all the things necessary to cause us to distinctly recognize a body are present in it. But notice that while I speak and approach the fire, what remained of the taste is eliminated, the smell evaporates, the color alters, the shape is destroyed, the size increases, it becomes liquid and hot and one can hardly handle it, and when it is struck, no sound is emitted. Does the same wax remain after this change? We must admit that it remains; no one would judge otherwise. What then did I know so distinctly in this piece of wax? It could certainly be none of the things that the senses brought to my notice, since everything that falls under taste, smell, sight, touch, and hearing, is found to be changed, and yet the same wax remains.

Perhaps it was what I now think, namely, that this wax was not the sweetness of honey, or the agreeable scent of flowers, or the whiteness, or the shape, or the sound, but simply a body that a little while before appeared to me as perceptible under these forms, and that is now perceptible under others. But what, precisely, is it that I imagine when I form such conceptions? Let us attentively consider this, and, taking away all that does not belong to the wax, let us see what remains. Certainly nothing remains except a certain extended thing that is flexible and movable. But what is the meaning of "flexible" and "movable"? Is it not that I imagine that this round piece of wax is able to become square and to pass from a square to a triangular shape? No, certainly it is not that, since I imagine it admits of an infinity of similar changes, and I nevertheless do not know how to encompass this infinity by my imagination, and consequently this conception I have of the wax is not brought about by the faculty of imagination. What now is this extension? Is it not also unknown? For it becomes greater when the wax is melted, greater when it is boiled, and still greater when the heat increases. And I would not conceive rightly what wax is, if I did not think that even this piece that we are considering is capable of receiving more variations in extension than I have ever imagined. We must then grant that I could not even understand through the imagination what this piece of wax is, and that it is my mind alone that perceives it. I am speaking of this piece of wax in particular, but for wax in general it is even clearer. But what is this piece of wax that cannot be understood except by the mind? It is certainly the same wax that I see, touch, imagine; in short, it is the same wax that I have always believed it to be from the beginning. But what must particularly be observed is that its perception is not an act of vision, touch, or imagination (and has never been such, although it may have previously appeared to be so), but only an intuition of the mind, which may be imperfect and confused as it was formerly, or clear and distinct as it is at present, according to the degree of attention I pay to the elements that are found in it, and of which it is composed. . . .

But what shall I say of this mind—that is, of myself (for up to this point I do not admit anything else in me but mind)? What then am I, who seem to perceive this piece of wax so distinctly? Do I not know myself, not only with much more truth and certainty, but also with much more distinctness and clearness [than I know the wax]? For if I judge that the wax is or exists from the fact that I see it, it certainly follows much more clearly that I myself exist from the fact that I see it. For it may be that what I see is not really wax, and it may also be that I do not possess eyes with which to see anything; but it cannot be that when I see or *think* I see (for I no longer make the distinction), that I myself who think am nothing. So if I judge that the wax exists from the fact that I touch it, the same thing will follow—namely, that I am. And if I judge that my imagination, or some other cause, whatever it is, persuades me that the wax exists, I will still draw the same conclusion. What I have here said of wax may be applied to all other things external to me. Furthermore, if the perception of wax has seemed to me clearer and more distinct after sight or touch (and many other causes as well) have made it quite evident to me, how much more distinctly must I now know myself, since all the reasons that contribute to the knowledge of wax, or any other body whatseover, are even better proofs of the nature of my mind. . . .

### Meditation V. Of the Essence of Material Things; and Again of God, That He Exists

. . . It is certain that the idea of God is in me—that is, the idea of a supremely perfect being—no less than the idea of any shape or number. I do not know any less clearly and distinctly that eternal existence pertains to this nature, than I know that everything I am able to demonstrate about some shape or number truly pertains to the nature of that shape or number. Therefore, even if everything that I concluded in the preceding meditations were false, I ought to be at least as certain of the existence of God as I have ever been of the truths of mathematics, which concern only numbers and shapes.

This is not at first obvious, since it appears to be a sophism.[2] For being accustomed in all other things to make a distinction between existence and essence, I easily persuade myself that the existence can be separated from the essence of God, and that we can thus conceive God as not actually existing. But when I think of it with more attention, I clearly see that existence can no more be separated from the essence of God, than having its three angles equal two right angles can be separated from the essence of a triangle, or than the idea of a mountain can be separated from the idea of a valley. And so it is no less repugnant to conceive of a God (that is, a supremely perfect being) lacking existence (that is, lacking a certain perfection), than to conceive of a mountain lacking a valley.

But although I cannot really conceive of God without existence any more than a mountain without a valley, still from the fact that I conceive of a mountain with a valley, it does not follow that a mountain exists in the world. Similarly, although I conceive of God as possessing existence, it would seem not to follow that God exists. For my thought does not impose any necessity upon things; and just as I may imagine a winged horse even though no horse with wings exists, so I could perhaps attribute existence to God, even though no God exists.

But a sophism is concealed in this objection. For from the fact that I cannot conceive a mountain without a valley, it does not follow that there is any mountain or any valley in existence, but only that the mountain and the valley, whether they exist or not, cannot in any way be separated from one another. But from the fact that I cannot conceive God without existence, it follows that existence is inseparable from him, and thus that he really exists. This is not because my thought can bring it about, or impose any necessity on things; on the contrary, the necessity lying in the thing itself—that is, the necessity of the existence of God—determines me to think in this way. For it is not within my power to think of God without existence (that is, a supremely perfect being without a supreme perfection), although it is in my power to imagine a horse either with or without wings. . . .

### Meditation VI. Of the Existence of Material Things, and of the Real Distinction between the Soul and the Body of Man

. . . Now that I am beginning to know myself better, and to discover more clearly the author of my being, I do not in truth think that I should rashly admit everything that the senses seem to teach me. On the other hand, I do not think that I should doubt everything.

First of all, since I know that everything that I apprehend clearly and distinctly can be created by God as I apprehend it, it is enough that I am able to apprehend one thing apart from another clearly and distinctly in order to be certain that the one is different from the other, since they can be made to exist separately, at least by the omnipotence of God. The question of what power makes this separation is irrelevant to the judgment that they are different. Therefore, because I know certainly that I exist, and meanwhile do not judge that anything else necessarily pertains to my nature or essence, except that I am a thinking thing, I rightly conclude that my essence consists solely in the fact that I am a thinking thing. And although possibly (or rather, *certainly,* as I will say in a moment) I possess a body with which I am very intimately joined, yet because, on the one hand, I have a clear and distinct idea of myself insofar as I am only a thinking and nonextended thing, and, on the other hand, I have a distinct idea of body, insofar it is only an extended and nonthinking thing, it is certain that this "I" is entirely and absolutely distinct from my body and can exist without it.

I further find in myself faculties employing modes of thinking peculiar to themselves—namely, the faculties of imagination and sensation—without which I can easily conceive myself clearly and distinctly as a complete being. On the other hand, they cannot be so conceived apart from me (that is, without an intelligent substance in which they reside), for in their formal concept, some kind of intellection is involved, from which I infer that they are distinct from me, as the modes of a thing are distinct from the thing itself. I observe also in me certain other faculties (such as changing positions, assuming different shapes, and so on) that cannot be conceived, any more than can the preceding, apart from some substance to which they are attached, and consequently cannot exist without it. But it is very clear that these faculties, if they really exist, must be attached to some corporeal or extended substance, and not to an intelligent substance, since, in the clear and distinct conception of these, some sort of extension is present but no intellection at all. There is certainly also in me a certain passive faculty of perception (that is, of receiving and recognizing the ideas of things that can be perceived), but this would be useless to me if there were not an active faculty, either in me or in something else, capable of forming and producing these ideas. But this active faculty cannot exist in me, because it does not presuppose thought, and because these ideas are often produced in me without my contributing in any way to them, and often even against my will. It is thus necessarily the case that this active faculty resides in some substance different from me, which contains, either formally or eminently,[3] all the reality that is objectively in the ideas[4] produced by this faculty. . . . And this substance is either a body—that is, a corporeal nature that contains formally everything that is objectively in these ideas—or it is God himself, or some other creature that is more noble than body and contains these ideas eminently. But since God is not a deceiver, it is very clear that he does not communicate these ideas immediately from himself, or through the intervention of some creature in which their reality is contained not formally but only eminently. For since God has given me no faculty to recognize that this is the case, but, on the other hand, a very great inclination to believe that they are conveyed to me by corporeal objects, I do not see how he could be defended from the accusation of deceit if these ideas were produced by causes other than corporeal objects. Therefore, corporeal things exist. However, they are perhaps not exactly what we grasp by the senses, since this grasp by the senses is often very obscure and confused. But we must at least admit that all things that I conceive in them clearly and distinctly—that is, all things that, generally speaking, are included in the subject matter of pure mathematics—are truly to be recognized as external objects. . . .

There is nothing that my nature teaches me more vividly than that I have a body that is adversely affected when I feel pain, that needs food or drink when I experience hunger and thirst, and so on. And I cannot doubt that there is some truth in all this.

Nature also teaches me by these sensations of pain, hunger, thirst, and so on, that I am not only lodged in my body as a sailor in a ship, but that I am very closely united to it and, so to speak, so intermingled with it that I seem to compose a single thing with it. For if that were not the case, when my body is hurt, I, who am merely a thinking thing, would not feel pain, for I would perceive this wound only by the understanding, just as a sailor perceives by sight when something is damaged in his ship. And when my body needs drink or food, I would clearly understand the fact without being warned of it by confused feelings of hunger and thirst. For all these sensations of hunger, thirst, pain, and so on, are in fact nothing other than certain confused modes of thought produced by the union and apparent intermingling of mind and body.

---

▶ NOTES

1. Archimedes (about 287–212 B.C.E.) was a Greek mathematician and inventor. [D. C. ABEL, EDITOR]
2. *sophism:* a plausible but incorrect argument intended to deceive [D. C. ABEL]
3. A substance contains something *formally* if it possesses that thing in the *same form* as in the effect it produces; it contains something *eminently* if it possesses that thing in a form *higher* than the one it produces in the effect. For example, a tree as a cause of another tree contains "treeness" formally, but God as the cause of a tree contains "treeness" eminently. [D. C. ABEL]
4. *objectively in the ideas:* in the ideas as representing the object (subject matter) of the ideas [D. C. ABEL]

Abel
Discourses

Theories of Knowledge

David Hume
An Enquiry Concerning
Human Understanding
(selection 1)

© McGraw–Hill, Inc., 1994

81

# An Enquiry Concerning Human Understanding

David Hume

David Hume was born in 1711 in Edinburgh, Scotland. His family wanted him to become a lawyer, but he found himself more interested in liberal arts than law. After three years at the University of Edinburgh (1723–1725), Hume withdrew to study literature, history, and philosophy privately at home. His intensive study took its toll on his health, and in 1729 he nearly had a nervous breakdown. In 1734 Hume went to Bristol, England, to take a job as a clerk for a sugar company. But he disliked the life of commerce and soon resigned his job. Hume then lived in France three years, studying philosophy. In 1744 he applied for a position in moral philosophy at the University of Edinburgh. Not chosen for the post, he spent the next several years in various occupations in England and abroad. Hume lived in Edinburgh from 1751 to 1763 and then went to Paris, where he served as secretary to the British Embassy for three years. Upon his return, he first lived in London but then moved back to Edinburgh, where he died in 1776.

Hume's major works are *A Treatise of Human Nature* (three volumes, 1739–1740), *An Enquiry Concerning Human Understanding* (1748; originally entitled *Philosophical Essays Concerning Human Understanding,* but renamed in the 1758 edition), *An Enquiry Concerning the Principles of Morals* (1751), *History of England* (six volumes, 1754–1762), and *Dialogues Concerning Natural Religion* (published posthumously, 1779).

Our reading is from the *Enquiry Concerning Human Understanding*. Hume begins by distinguishing two kinds of perceptions of the mind: impressions and ideas. *Impressions* consist of direct sense experiences of things outside us (sensations) or inside us (passions and emotions); *ideas* are copies of such impressions. Impressions are distinguished from ideas by their greater "force and vivacity"; hearing a sound is an impression, whereas recalling the sound is an idea. Some ideas (for example, a gold mountain) are not direct copies of a particular impression, but modifications or combinations of impressions (gold and a mountain). To clarify an idea, we need simply go back to the impression(s) from which it derives.

Hume next inquires about our knowledge of "matters of fact" (things that could be otherwise than they are). He observes that we rely on the notion of cause and effect when we go beyond the matters of fact provided by impressions and memories of impressions. But how do we *know* that one thing is caused by another? Judgments of causality are based on experience; when we see that event A is followed regularly by event B, we infer that A causes B and that if A occurs in the future, it will be followed by B. But what justifies this inference? It is not based on impressions—for while we do have impressions of A and B as successive events, we have no impression of a third entity, a "cause," which links A and B. Consequently, we can *never know* that there is such a thing as causality. Hume argues that our belief in causality results not from a reasoning process, but from the unavoidable human tendency to believe that two events we experience as constantly conjoined are related as cause and effect.

▼

### Section II: Of the Origin of Ideas

Everyone will readily allow that there is a considerable difference between the perceptions of the mind when a man feels the pain of excessive heat or the pleasure of moderate warmth, and when he afterwards recalls to his memory this sensation or anticipates it by his imagination. These faculties may mimic or copy the perceptions of the senses, but they never can entirely reach the force and vivacity of the original sentiment.[1] The utmost we say of them, even when they operate with greatest vigour, is that they represent their object in so lively a manner that we could *almost* say we feel or see it. But, except the mind be disordered by disease or madness, they never can arrive at such a pitch of vivacity as to render these perceptions altogether undistinguishable. All the colours of poetry, however splendid, can never paint natural objects in such a manner as to make the description be taken for a real landscape. The most lively thought is still inferior to the dullest sensation.

We may observe a like distinction to run through all the other perceptions of the mind. A man in a fit of anger is actuated in a very different manner from one who only thinks of that emotion. If you tell me that any person is in love, I easily understand your meaning and form a just conception of his situation, but never can mistake that conception for the real disorders and agitations of the passion. When we reflect on our past sentiments and affections, our thought is a faithful mirror and copies its objects truly, but the colours which it employs are faint and dull in comparison of those in which our original perceptions were clothed. It requires no nice discernment or metaphysical head to mark the distinction between them.

Here therefore we may divide all the perceptions of the mind into two classes or species, which are distinguished by their different degrees of force and vivacity. The less forcible and lively are commonly denominated *thoughts* or *ideas*. The other species want a name in our language, and in most others; I suppose, because it was not requisite for any but philosophical purposes, to rank them under a general term or appellation. Let us, therefore, use a little freedom and call them *impressions*, employing that word in a sense somewhat different from the usual. By the term *impression*, then, I mean all our more lively perceptions, when we hear, or see, or feel, or love, or hate, or desire, or will. And impressions are distinguished from ideas, which are the less lively perceptions, of which we are conscious when we reflect on any of those sensations or movements above mentioned.

Nothing, at first view, may seem more unbounded than the thought of man, which not only escapes all human power and authority, but is not even restrained within the limits of nature and reality. To form monsters and join incongruous shapes and appearances costs the imagination no more trouble than to conceive the most natural and familiar objects. And while the body is confined to one planet, along which it creeps with pain and difficulty; the thought can in an instant transport us into the most distant regions of the universe; or even beyond the universe, into the unbounded chaos, where nature is supposed to lie in total confusion. What never was seen, or heard of, may yet be conceived; nor is any thing beyond the power of thought, except what implies an absolute contradiction.

But though our thought seems to possess this unbounded liberty, we shall find, upon a nearer examination, that it is really confined within very narrow limits and that all this creative power of the mind amounts to no more than the faculty of compounding, transposing, augmenting, or diminishing the materials afforded us by the senses and experience. When we think of a golden mountain, we only join two consistent ideas, *gold* and *mountain,* with which we were formerly acquainted. A virtuous horse we can conceive because, from our own feeling, we can conceive virtue; and this we may unite to the figure and shape of a horse, which is an animal familiar to us. In short, all the materials of thinking are derived either from our outward or inward sentiment: the mixture and composition of these belongs alone to the mind and will. Or, to express myself in philosophical language, all our ideas or more feeble perceptions are copies of our impressions or more lively ones.

To prove this, the two following arguments will, I hope, be sufficient. First, when we analyze our thoughts or ideas, however compounded or sublime, we always find that they resolve themselves into such simple ideas as were copied from a precedent[2] feeling or sentiment. Even those ideas which, at first view, seem the most wide of this origin, are found, upon a nearer scrutiny, to be derived from it. The idea of God, as meaning an infinitely intelligent, wise, and good Being, arises from reflecting on the operations of our own mind and augmenting, without limit, those qualities of goodness and wisdom. We may prosecute[3] this enquiry to what length we please; where we shall always find that every idea which we examine is copied from a similar impression. Those who would assert that this position is not universally true nor without exception, have only one, and that an easy method of refuting it; by producing that idea, which, in their opinion, is not derived from this source. It will then be incumbent on us, if we would maintain our doctrine, to produce the impression, or lively perception, which corresponds to it.

Secondly, if it happen from a defect of the organ that a man is not susceptible of any species of sensation, we always find that he is as little susceptible of the correspondent ideas. A blind man can form no notion of colours; a deaf man of sounds. Restore either of them that sense in which he is deficient; by opening this new inlet for his sensations, you also open an inlet for the ideas; and he finds no difficulty in conceiving these objects. . . .

When we entertain, therefore, any suspicion that a philosophical term is employed without any meaning or idea (as is but too frequent), we need but enquire, *from what impression is that supposed idea derived?* And if it be impossible to assign any, this will serve to confirm our suspicion. By bringing ideas into so clear a light we may reasonably hope to remove all dispute which may arise concerning their nature and reality. . . .

### Section IV: Sceptical Doubts Concerning the Operations of the Understanding

**Part I** All the objects of human reason or enquiry may naturally be divided into two kinds, to wit, *relations of ideas* and *matters of fact.* Of the first kind are the sciences of geometry, algebra, and arithmetic; and in short, every

Abel
Discourses

Theories of Knowledge

David Hume
An Enquiry Concerning
Human Understanding
(selection 1)

© McGraw–Hill, Inc., 1994

affirmation which is either intuitively or demonstratively certain. *That the square of the hypothenuse is equal to the square of the two sides* is a proposition which expresses a relation between these figures. *That three times five is equal to the half of thirty* expresses a relation between these numbers. Propositions of this kind are discoverable by the mere operation of thought, without dependence on what is anywhere existent in the universe. Though there never were a circle or triangle in nature, the truths demonstrated by Euclid[4] would for ever retain their certainty and evidence.

Matters of fact, which are the second objects of human reason, are not ascertained in the same manner; nor is our evidence of their truth, however great, of a like nature with the foregoing. The contrary of every matter of fact is still possible; because it can never imply a contradiction and is conceived by the mind with the same facility and distinctness, as if ever so conformable to reality. *That the sun will not rise tomorrow* is no less intelligible a proposition and implies no more contradiction than the affirmation, *that it will rise*. We should in vain, therefore, attempt to demonstrate its falsehood. Were it demonstratively false, it would imply a contradiction and could never be distinctly conceived by the mind.

It may, therefore, be a subject worthy of curiosity, to enquire what is the nature of that evidence which assures us of any real existence and matter of fact, beyond the present testimony of our senses or the records of our memory. This part of philosophy, it is observable, has been little cultivated, either by the ancients or moderns; and therefore our doubts and errors, in the prosecution of so important an enquiry, may be the more excusable, while we march through such difficult paths without any guide or direction. They may even prove useful, by exciting curiosity and destroying that implicit faith and security which is the bane of all reasoning and free enquiry. The discovery of defects in the common philosophy, if any such there be, will not, I presume, be a discouragement, but rather an incitement, as is usual, to attempt something more full and satisfactory than has yet been proposed to the public.

All reasonings concerning matter of fact seem to be founded on the relation of *cause and effect*. By means of that relation alone we can go beyond the evidence of our memory and senses. If you were to ask a man why he believes any matter of fact, which is absent; for instance, that his friend is in the country, or in France; he would give you a reason; and this reason would be some other fact; as a letter received from him, or the knowledge of his former resolutions and promises. A man finding a watch or any other machine in a desert island would conclude that there had once been men in that island. All our reasonings concerning fact are of the same nature. And here it is constantly supposed that there is a connexion between the present fact and that which is inferred from it. Were there nothing to bind them together, the inference would be entirely precarious. The hearing of an articulate voice and rational discourse in the dark assures us of the presence of some person. Why? Because these are the effects of the

Abel
Discourses

Theories of Knowledge

David Hume
An Enquiry Concerning
Human Understanding
(selection 1)

© McGraw–Hill, Inc., 1994

85

human make and fabric, and closely connected with it. If we anatomize all the other reasonings of this nature, we shall find that they are founded on the relation of cause and effect, and that this relation is either near or remote, direct, or collateral. Heat and light are collateral effects of fire, and the one effect may justly be inferred from the other.

If we would satisfy ourselves, therefore, concerning the nature of that evidence which assures us of matters of fact, we must enquire how we arrive at the knowledge of cause and effect.

I shall venture to affirm, as a general proposition which admits of no exception, that the knowledge of this relation is not, in any instance, attained by reasonings a priori,[5] but arises entirely from experience, when we find that any particular objects are constantly conjoined with each other. Let an object be presented to a man of ever so strong natural reason and abilities; if that object be entirely new to him, he will not be able, by the most accurate examination of its sensible[6] qualities, to discover any of its causes or effects. Adam, though his rational faculties be supposed, at the very first, entirely perfect, could not have inferred from the fluidity and transparency of water that it would suffocate him, or from the light and warmth of fire that it would consume him. No object ever discovers, by the qualities which appear to the senses, either the causes which produced it, or the effects which will arise from it; nor can our reason, unassisted by experience, ever draw any inference concerning real existence and matter of fact.

This proposition *that causes and effects are discoverable, not by reason but by experience* will readily be admitted with regard to such objects as we remember to have once been altogether unknown to us; since we must be conscious of the utter inability, which we then lay under, of foretelling what would arise from them. Present two smooth pieces of marble to a man who has no tincture of natural philosophy;[7] he will never discover that they will adhere together in such a manner as to require great force to separate them in a direct line, while they make so small a resistance to a lateral pressure. Such events, as bear little analogy to the common course of nature, are also readily confessed to be known only by experience; nor does any man imagine that the explosion of gunpowder or the attraction of a loadstone could ever be discovered by arguments a priori. In like manner, when an effect is supposed to depend upon an intricate machinery or secret[8] structure of parts, we make no difficulty in attributing all our knowledge of it to experience. Who will assert that he can give the ultimate reason why milk or bread is proper nourishment for a man, not for a lion or a tiger?

But the same truth may not appear, at first sight, to have the same evidence with regard to events which have become familiar to us from our first appearance in the world, which bear a close analogy to the whole course of nature, and which are supposed to depend on the simple qualities of objects, without any secret structure of parts. We are apt to imagine

Abel
Discourses

Theories of Knowledge

David Hume
An Enquiry Concerning
Human Understanding
(selection 1)

© McGraw–Hill, Inc., 1994

that we could discover these effects by the mere operation of our reason, without experience. We fancy that were we brought on a sudden into this world, we could at first have inferred that one billiard ball would communicate motion to another upon impulse; and that we needed not to have waited for the event, in order to pronounce with certainty concerning it. Such is the influence of custom, that, where it is strongest, it not only covers our natural ignorance, but even conceals itself and seems not to take place, merely because it is found in the highest degree.

But to convince us that all the laws of nature, and all the operations of bodies without exception, are known only by experience, the following reflections may, perhaps, suffice. Were any object presented to us, and were we required to pronounce concerning the effect which will result from it, without consulting past observation; after what manner, I beseech you, must the mind proceed in this operation? It must invent or imagine some event which it ascribes to the object as its effect; and it is plain that this invention must be entirely arbitrary. The mind can never possibly find the effect in the supposed cause, by the most accurate scrutiny and examination. For the effect is totally different from the cause and consequently can never be discovered in it. Motion in the second billiard ball is a quite distinct event from motion in the first; nor is there anything in the one to suggest the smallest hint of the other. A stone or piece of metal raised into the air, and left without any support, immediately falls: but to consider the matter a priori, is there anything we discover in this situation which can beget the idea of a downward, rather than an upward, or any other motion, in the stone or metal?

And as the first imagination or invention of a particular effect, in all natural operations, is arbitrary, where we consult not experience; so must we also esteem the supposed tie or connexion between the cause and effect, which binds them together and renders it impossible that any other effect could result from the operation of that cause. When I see, for instance, a billiard ball moving in a straight line towards another; even suppose motion in the second ball should by accident be suggested to me, as the result of their contact or impulse; may I not conceive that a hundred different events might as well follow from that cause? May not both these balls remain at absolute rest? May not the first ball return in a straight line or leap off from the second in any line or direction? All these suppositions are consistent and conceivable. Why then should we give the preference to one, which is no more consistent or conceivable than the rest? All our reasonings a priori will never be able to show us any foundation for this preference.

In a word, then, every effect is a distinct event from its cause. It could not, therefore, be discovered in the cause, and the first invention or conception of it, a priori, must be entirely arbitrary. And even after it is suggested, the conjunction of it with the cause must appear equally arbitrary; since there are always many other effects, which to reason must seem fully

Abel
Discourses

Theories of Knowledge

David Hume
An Enquiry Concerning
Human Understanding
(selection 1)

© McGraw–Hill, Inc., 1994

87

as consistent and natural. In vain, therefore, should we pretend to determine any single event, or infer any cause or effect, without the assistance of observation and experience. . . .

**Part II** But we have not yet attained any tolerable satisfaction with regard to the question first proposed. Each solution still gives rise to a new question as difficult as the foregoing, and leads us on to farther enquiries. When it is asked, *What is the nature of all our reasonings concerning matter of fact?* the proper answer seems to be that they are founded on the relation of cause and effect. When again it is asked, *What is the foundation of all our reasonings and conclusions concerning that relation?* it may be replied in one word, experience. But if we still carry on our sifting humour[9] and ask, *What is the foundation of all conclusions from experience?* this implies a new question, which may be of more difficult solution and explication. Philosophers that give themselves airs of superior wisdom and sufficiency have a hard task when they encounter persons of inquisitive dispositions who push them from every corner to which they retreat, and who are sure at last to bring them to some dangerous dilemma. The best expedient to prevent this confusion is to be modest in our pretensions, and even to discover the difficulty ourselves before it is objected to us. By this means, we may make a kind of merit of our very ignorance.

I shall content myself, in this section, with an easy task and shall pretend[10] only to give a negative answer to the question here proposed. I say then, that even after we have experience of the operations of cause and effect, our conclusions from that experience are *not* founded on reasoning or any process of the understanding. This answer we must endeavour both to explain and to defend.

It must certainly be allowed that nature has kept us at a great distance from all her secrets and has afforded us only the knowledge of a few superficial qualities of objects, while she conceals from us those powers and principles on which the influence of those objects entirely depends. . . . If a body of like colour and consistence with that bread, which we have formerly eaten, be presented to us, we make no scruple of repeating the experiment, and foresee, with certainty, like nourishment and support. Now this is a process of the mind or thought, of which I would willingly know the foundation. It is allowed on all hands that there is no known connexion between the sensible qualities and the secret powers; and consequently, that the mind is not led to form such a conclusion concerning their constant and regular conjunction, by anything which it knows of their nature. As to past *experience*, it can be allowed to give *direct* and *certain* information of those precise objects only, and that precise period of time, which fell under its cognizance: but why this experience should be extended to future times and to other objects which, for aught we know, may be only in appearance similar; this is the main question on which I would insist. The bread which I formerly ate nourished me; that is, a body of such sensible qualities was,

Abel
Discourses

Theories of Knowledge

David Hume
An Enquiry Concerning
Human Understanding
(selection 1)

© McGraw–Hill, Inc., 1994

at that time, endued with such secret powers. But does it follow that other bread must also nourish me at another time, and that like sensible qualities must always be attended with like secret powers? The consequence seems nowise necessary. At least it must be acknowledged that there is here a consequence drawn by the mind; that there is a certain step taken; a process of thought and an inference which wants to be explained. These two propositions are far from being the same, *I have found that such an object has always been attended with such an effect,* and *I foresee that other objects which are in appearance similar will be attended with similar effects.* I shall allow, if you please, that the one proposition may justly be inferred from the other; I know, in fact, that it always is inferred. But if you insist that the inference is made by a chain of reasoning, I desire you to produce that reasoning. The connexion between these propositions is not intuitive. There is required a medium[11] which may enable the mind to draw such an inference, if indeed it be drawn by reasoning and argument. What that medium is, I must confess, passes my comprehension; and it is incumbent on those to produce it, who assert that it really exists and is the origin of all our conclusions concerning matter of fact. . . .

When a new object, endowed with similar sensible qualities, is produced, we expect similar powers and forces and look for a like effect. From a body of like colour and consistence with bread we expect like nourishment and support. But this surely is a step or progress of the mind, which wants to be explained. When a man says, *I have found, in all past instances, such sensible qualities conjoined with such secret powers;* and when he says, *Similar sensible qualities will always be conjoined with similar secret powers,* he is not guilty of a tautology, nor are these propositions in any respect the same. You say that the one proposition is an inference from the other. But you must confess that the inference is not intuitive; neither is it demonstrative. Of what nature is it, then? To say it is experimental, is begging the question. For all inferences from experience suppose, as their foundation, that the future will resemble the past and that similar powers will be conjoined with similar sensible qualities. If there be any suspicion that the course of nature may change and that the past may be no rule for the future, all experience becomes useless and can give rise to no inference or conclusion. It is impossible, therefore, that any arguments from experience can prove this resemblance of the past to the future, since all these arguments are founded on the supposition of that resemblance. Let the course of things be allowed hitherto ever so regular; that alone, without some new argument or inference, proves not that, for the future, it will continue so. In vain do you pretend to have learned the nature of bodies from your past experience. Their secret nature, and consequently all their effects and influence, may change without any change in their sensible qualities. This happens sometimes and with regard to some objects: Why may it not happen always and with regard to all objects? What logic, what process of argument secures you against this supposition? My practice, you say, refutes my doubts. But you mistake the purport of my question. As an agent, I am quite satisfied in the point; but as a philosopher, who has some share of curiosity, I will not say scepticism, I want to learn the foundation of this inference. No reading, no enquiry has yet been able to remove my difficulty or give me satisfaction in a matter of such importance. Can I do better than propose the difficulty to the public, even though, perhaps, I have small hopes of obtaining a solution? We shall at least, by this means, be sensible[12] of our ignorance, if we do not augment our knowledge. . . .

### Section V: Sceptical Solution of These Doubts

**Part I** . . . Suppose a person, though endowed with the strongest faculties of reason and reflection, to be brought on a sudden into this world; he would, indeed, immediately observe a continual succession of objects, and one event following another; but he would not be able to discover anything farther. He would not, at first, by any reasoning, be able to reach the idea of cause and effect; since the particular powers by which all natural operations are performed never appear to the senses; nor is it reasonable to conclude, merely because one event, in one instance, precedes another, that therefore the one is the cause, the other the effect. Their conjunction may be arbitrary and casual. There may be no reason to infer the existence of one from the appearance of the other. And in a word, such a person, without more experience, could never employ his conjecture or reasoning concerning any matter of fact, or be assured of anything beyond what was immediately present to his memory and senses.

Suppose, again, that he has acquired more experience and has lived so long in the world as to have observed familiar objects or events to be constantly conjoined together; what is the consequence of this experience? He immediately infers the existence of one object from the appearance of the other. Yet he has not, by all his experience, acquired any idea or knowledge of the secret power by which the one object produces the other; nor is it by any process of reasoning [that] he is engaged to draw this inference. But still he finds himself determined to draw it: And though he should be convinced that his understanding has no part in the operation, he would nevertheless continue in the same course of thinking. There is some other principle which determines him to form such a conclusion.

This principle is custom or habit. For wherever the repetition of any particular act or operation produces a propensity to renew the same act or operation, without being impelled by any reasoning or process of the understanding, we always say that this propensity is the effect of *custom*. By employing that word, we pretend not to have given the ultimate reason of such a propensity. We only point out a principle of human nature which is universally acknowledged and which is well known by its effects. Perhaps we can push our enquiries no farther or pretend to give the cause of this cause, but must rest contented with it as the ultimate principle which we can assign of all our conclusions from experience. It is sufficient satisfaction that we can go so far, without repining at the narrowness of our faculties because they will carry us no farther. And it is certain we here advance a very intelligible proposition at least, if not a true one, when we assert that, after the constant conjunction of two objects—heat and flame, for instance, weight and solidity—we are determined by custom alone to expect the one from the appearance of the other. This hypothesis seems even the only one which explains the difficulty why we draw, from a thousand instances, an inference which we are not able to draw from one instance that is in no respect different from them. Reason is incapable of any such variation. The conclusions which it draws from considering one circle are the same which it would form upon surveying all the circles in the universe. But no man, having seen only one body move after being impelled by another, could infer that every other body will move after a like impulse. All inferences from experience, therefore, are effects of custom, not of reasoning.

Custom, then, is the great guide of human life. It is that principle alone which renders our experience useful to us and makes us expect, for the future, a similar train of events with those which have appeared in the past. Without the influence of custom, we should be entirely ignorant of every matter of fact beyond what is immediately present to the memory and senses. We should never know how to adjust means to ends, or to employ our natural powers in the production of any effect. There would be an end at once of all action, as well as of the chief part of speculation.

But here it may be proper to remark that though our conclusions from experience carry us beyond our memory and senses and assure us of matters of fact which happened in the most distant places and most remote ages, yet some fact must always be present to the senses or memory, from which we may first proceed in drawing these conclusions. A man who should find in a desert country the remains of pompous[13] buildings would conclude that the country had, in ancient times, been cultivated by civilized inhabitants; but did nothing of this nature occur to him, he could never form such an inference. We learn the events of former ages from history; but then we must peruse the volumes in which this instruction is contained, and thence carry up our inferences from one testimony to another, till we arrive at the eyewitnesses and spectators of these distant events. In a word, if we proceed not upon some fact present to the memory or senses, our reasonings would be merely hypothetical; and however the particular links might be connected with each other, the whole chain of inferences would have nothing to support it, nor could we ever, by its means, arrive at the knowledge of any real existence. If I ask why you believe any particular matter of fact which you relate, you must tell me some reason; and this reason will be some other fact, connected with it. But as you cannot proceed after this manner *in infinitum,*[14] you must at last terminate in some fact which is present to your memory or senses; or must allow that your belief is entirely without foundation.

Abel
Discourses

Theories of Knowledge

David Hume
An Enquiry Concerning
Human Understanding
(selection 1)

© McGraw–Hill, Inc., 1994

91

What, then, is the conclusion of the whole matter? A simple one; though, it must be confessed, pretty remote from the common theories of philosophy. All belief of matter of fact or real existence is derived merely from some object present to the memory or senses, and a customary conjunction between that and some other object. Or in other words; having found, in many instances, that any two kinds of objects—flame and heat, snow and cold—have always been conjoined together; if flame or snow be presented anew to the senses, the mind is carried by custom to expect heat or cold and to *believe* that such a quality does exist and will discover itself upon a nearer approach. This belief is the necessary result of placing the mind in such circumstances. It is an operation of the soul, when we are so situated, as unavoidable as to feel the passion of love when we receive benefits, or hatred, when we meet with injuries. All these operations are a species of natural instincts, which no reasoning or process of the thought and understanding is able either to produce or to prevent.

▶ NOTES

1. *sentiment:* perception [D.C.A., ed.]
2. *precedent:* prior [D.C.A.]
3. *prosecute:* pursue [D.C.A.]
4. Euclid, who flourished in about 300 B.C.E., was a Greek geometer. [D.C.A.]
5. *a priori:* based on abstract reasoning, independent of experience (literally, in Latin, "from what comes earlier") [D.C.A.]
6. *sensible:* able to be sensed [D.C.A.]
7. *natural philosophy:* the philosophy of nature, i.e., natural science [D.C.A.]
8. *secret:* unseen [D.C.A.]
9. *sifting humour:* questioning frame of mind [D.C.A.]
10. *pretend:* undertake [D.C.A.]
11. *medium:* basis for an inference [D.C.A.]
12. *sensible:* aware [D.C.A.]
13. *pompous:* magnificent [D.C.A.]
14. *in infinitum:* to infinity (Latin) [D.C.A.]

# Critique of Pure Reason

Immanuel Kant

Immanuel Kant was born in 1724 in Königsberg, Prussia, where he spent his entire life. As a boy he attended the Collegium Fridericanum, a school run by the Pietists (the Lutheran sect to which his family belonged). In 1740 he enrolled in the University of Königsberg, where he studied a wide variety of subjects, including theology, philosophy, mathematics, physics, and medicine. He withdrew from the university in 1747 to support himself by working as a private tutor for various families in eastern Prussia. He resumed his studies in 1754 and completed his degree the following year. He then became a lecturer at the University of Königsberg, teaching such diverse subjects as mathematics, geography, mineralogy, and philosophy. Fifteen years later he was appointed Professor of Logic and Metaphysics. His writings—especially his monumental *Critique of Pure Reason* (1781)—brought him increasing fame, and students came from afar to hear him lecture. In 1797 he stopped lecturing, but he continued to write. He died in Königsberg in 1804 at the age of seventy-nine.

Kant's principal works, in addition to the *Critique of Pure Reason,* are *Prolegomena to Any Future Metaphysics* (1783), *Fundamental Principles of the Metaphysics of Morals* (1785), *Critique of Practical Reason* (1788), and *Critique of Judgment* (1790).

Our reading is taken from Kant's second edition of the *Critique of Pure Reason,* published in 1787. Kant's project in this book is to investigate how much we can know by "pure reason" (reason itself, apart from any experience). In his Preface, Kant observes that we typically assume that our knowledge (cognition) must conform to objects—that when we know something, our mind must match the way the objects are. If this assumption is correct, it would be impossible to have any knowledge of objects a priori (prior to our experience of them). Kant rejects this assumption; he holds the converse, that *objects* must conform to our *knowledge*—that when we know something, objects must match the way our minds are. Objects conform to our way of receiving sense experience (intuition) and to our way of intellectually synthesizing this sense experience (thought). That is to say, our minds are constructed in such a way that we necessarily *sense* objects through the forms of "sensibility" (namely, space and time) and we necessarily *think* objects through certain "categories" (also called "concepts") of the understanding, such as causality and unity. This means that we can know certain things about objects a priori. For example, we know that we will experience them as existing in space and as being caused. But according to Kant, even though we know that objects will invariably *appear to us* in certain ways, we can never know how things are in *themselves.*

In his Introduction, Kant explains that a priori knowledge is characterized by necessity and universality. He then explains that some of our judgments (those in mathematics and metaphysics, for example) are not only a priori but synthetic. (A *synthetic* proposition adds something to a concept, while an *analytic* one does not.) Kant's doctrine about the structure of the mind is designed to explain how such synthetic a priori judgments are possible.

In the final two sections of our reading, Kant gives arguments to show that space and time (the forms of sensibility) are a priori, and explains that there are twelve categories of the understanding, corresponding to the twelve kinds of judgment.

▼

From Immanuel Kant, *Critique of Pure Reason,* trans. J. M. D. Meiklejohn. London, England: George Bell & Sons, 1878.

## Preface to the Second Edition

Whether the treatment of that portion of our knowledge that lies within the province of pure reason advances with that undeviating certainty that characterizes the progress of science, we shall be at no loss to determine. If we find those who are engaged in metaphysical[1] pursuits unable to come to an understanding of the method they ought to follow; if we find them, after the most elaborate preparations, invariably brought to a standstill before the goal is reached, and compelled to retrace their steps and strike into fresh paths, then we may then feel quite sure that they are far from having attained the certainty of scientific progress, and may rather be said to be merely groping about in the dark. In these circumstances we shall render an important service to reason if we succeed in simply indicating the path along which it must travel in order to arrive at any results—even if it should be found necessary to abandon many of those aims that, without reflection, have been proposed for its attainment. . . .

It has until now been assumed that our cognition must conform to the objects; but all attempts to ascertain anything about these objects a priori,[2] by means of concepts, and thus to extend the range of our knowledge, have been rendered abortive by this assumption. Let us then make the experiment whether we may not be more successful in metaphysics if we assume that . . . objects must conform to our cognition. This appears, at all events, to accord better with the *possibility* of our gaining the end we have in view—that is to say, arriving at the cognition of objects a priori, of determining something with respect to these objects before they are given to us. We here propose to do just what Copernicus[3] did in attempting to explain the celestial movements. When he found that he could make no progress by assuming that all the heavenly bodies revolved round the spectator, he reversed the process and tried the experiment of assuming that the spectator revolved, while the stars remained at rest. We may make the same experiment with regard to the intuition[4] of objects. If the intuition must conform to the nature of the objects, I do not see how we can know anything of them a priori. If, on the other hand, the object conforms to the nature of our faculty of intuition, I can then easily conceive the possibility of such an a priori knowledge. Now as I cannot rest in the mere intuitions, but—if they are to become cognitions—must refer them, as *representations*, to something, as *object*, and must determine the latter by means of the former, here again there are two courses open to me. *Either*, first, I may assume that the concepts by which I effect this determination conform to the object (and in this case I am reduced to the same perplexity as before); *or*, secondly, I may assume that the objects, or, which is the same thing, that *experience* (in which alone, as given objects, they are known) conforms to my concepts—and then I am at no loss how to proceed. For experience itself is a mode of cognition that requires understanding. Before objects are given to me (that is, a priori), I must presuppose in myself laws of the understanding that are expressed in concepts a priori. To these concepts, then, all the objects of experience must necessarily conform. . . .

## Introduction to the Second Edition

### I. On the Difference between Pure and Empirical Knowledge

That all our knowledge begins with experience there can be no doubt. For how is it possible that the faculty of cognition should be awakened into exercise otherwise than by means of objects that affect our senses, and partly of themselves produce representations, partly rouse our powers of understanding into activity, to compare, to connect, or to separate these, and so to convert the raw material of our sense impressions into a knowledge of objects, which is called experience? With respect to time, therefore, no knowledge of ours is antecedent to experience, but begins with it.

But, though all our knowledge *begins with* experience, it by no means follows that all knowledge *arises out of* experience. For, on the contrary, it is quite possible that our empirical knowledge is a compound of that which we receive through impressions and that which the faculty of cognition supplies from itself (sense impressions giving merely the *occasion*), an addition that we cannot distinguish from the original element given by sense, until long practice has made us attentive to it and skillful in separating it. It is therefore a question that requires close investigation, and not to be answered at first sight, whether there exists a knowledge altogether independent of experience, and even of all sense impressions. Knowledge of this kind is called a priori, in distinction from empirical knowledge, which has its sources a posteriori (that is, in experience).

But the expression "a priori" is not as yet definite enough to indicate adequately the whole meaning of the question stated above. For in speaking of knowledge that has its sources in experience, it is customary to say that this or that may be known a priori, because we do not derive this knowledge immediately from experience, but from a general rule, which, however, we have itself borrowed from experience. Thus, if a man undermined the foundation of his house, we say "He might know a priori that it would have fallen"—that is, he needed not to have waited for the experience that it did actually fall. But still, a priori, he could not know even this much. For, that bodies are heavy, and, consequently that they fall when their supports are taken away, must have been known to him previously, by means of experience.

By the term "a priori knowledge," therefore, we shall understand, not such as is independent of this or that kind of experience, but such as is absolutely so of all experience. Opposed to this is empirical knowledge, or that which is possible only a posteriori (that is, through experience). A priori knowledge is either pure or impure. Pure a priori knowledge is that with which no empirical element is included. For example, the proposition "Every change has a cause" is an a priori proposition, but impure, because change is a concept that can only be derived from experience.

## II. The Human Intellect, Even in an Unphilosophical State, Is in Possession of Certain A Priori Cognitions

The question now is by what *criterion* we may securely distinguish a pure from an empirical cognition. Experience no doubt teaches us that this or that object is constituted in such and such a manner, but not that it could not possibly exist otherwise. Now in the first place, if we have a proposition that contains the idea of necessity in its very concept, it is an a priori judgment; if, moreover, it is not derived from any other proposition, unless from one equally involving the idea of necessity, it is absolutely a priori. Secondly, an empirical judgment never exhibits strict and absolute, but only assumed and comparative universality (by induction); therefore, the most we can say is that, as far as we have observed up until now, there is no exception to this or that rule. If, on the other hand, a judgment carries with it strict and absolute universality (that is, admits of no possible exception), it is not derived from experience, but is valid absolutely a priori.

Empirical universality is, therefore, only an arbitrary extension of validity from what may be predicated of a proposition valid in most cases, to what is asserted of a proposition that holds good in all cases—as, for example, in the affirmation "All bodies are heavy." When, on the contrary, strict universality characterizes a judgment, it necessarily indicates another peculiar source of knowledge—namely, a faculty of a priori cognition. Necessity and strict universality, therefore, are infallible tests for distinguishing pure from empirical knowledge, and are inseparably connected with each other. But as in the use of these criteria the empirical limitation is sometimes more easily detected than the contingency[5] of the judgment, or the unlimited universality that we attach to a judgment is often a more convincing proof than its necessity, it may be advisable to use the criteria separately, each being by itself infallible.

The fact that in the sphere of human cognition, we have judgments that are necessary, and in the strictest sense universal, consequently pure a priori, it will be an easy matter to show. If we desire an example from the sciences, we need only take any proposition in mathematics. If we cast our eyes upon the commonest operations of the understanding, the proposition "Every change must have a cause" will amply serve our purpose. In the latter case, indeed, the concept of a cause so plainly involves the concept of a necessity of connection with an effect, and of a strict universality of the law, that the very notion of a cause would entirely disappear, if were we to derive it, as Hume[6] did, from a frequent association of what happens with what precedes it, and from a habit, originating from this, of connecting representations. The necessity inherent in the judgment would be merely subjective. Besides, without seeking for such examples of principles existing a priori in cognition, we might easily show that such principles are the indispensable basis of the possibility of experience itself, and consequently prove their existence a priori. For from where could our experience itself acquire certainty, if all the rules on which it depends were themselves empirical, and consequently fortuitous? No one, therefore, can admit the validity of the use of such rules as first principles. But, for the present, we may content ourselves with having established the fact that we do possess and exercise a faculty of pure a priori cognition; and, secondly, with having pointed out the proper tests of such cognition—namely, universality and necessity.

An a priori origin is manifest, however, not only in judgments, but even in concepts. For example, if we take away by degrees from our concepts of a body all that can be referred to mere sense experience—color, hardness or softness, weight, even impenetrability—the body will then vanish; but the space that it occupied still remains, and this it is utterly impossible to annihilate in thought. Again, if we take away, in like manner, from our empirical concept of any object, corporeal or incorporeal, all properties that mere experience has taught us to connect with it, still we cannot think away those through which we think it as substance, or adhering to substance, although our concept of substance is more determined than that of an object. Compelled, therefore, by that necessity with which the concept of substance forces itself upon us, we must confess that it has its seat in our faculty of a priori cognition. . . .

### IV. On the Difference between Analytic and Synthetic Judgments

In all judgments in which the relation of a subject to the predicate is thought (I mention affirmative judgments only here; the application to negative will be very easy), this relation is possible in two different ways. Either the predicate B belongs to the subject A, as something that is contained (though covertly) in the concept A; or the predicate B lies completely out of the concept A, although it stands in connection with it. In the first instance, I term the judgment *analytic;* in the second, *synthetic.* Analytic judgments (affirmative) are therefore those in which the connection of the predicate with the subject is thought through identity; those judgments in which this connection is thought without identity are called synthetic judgments. The former may be called *explicative,* the latter *augmentative* judgments; because the former add in the predicate nothing to the concept of the subject, but only analyze it into its constituent concepts, which were thought already in the subject, although in a confused manner; the latter add to our concepts of the subject a predicate that was not contained in it, and that no analysis could ever have discovered in it. For example, when I say "All bodies are extended," this is an analytic judgment. For I need not go beyond the concept of *body* in order to find extension connected with it, but merely analyze the concept—that is, become conscious of the manifold properties that I think in that concept—in order to discover this predicate in it: It is therefore an analytic judgment. On the other hand, when I say "All bodies are heavy," the predicate is something totally different from that which I think in the mere concept of a body. By the addition of such a predicate, therefore, it becomes a synthetic judgment.

Judgments of experience, as such, are always synthetic. For it would be absurd to think of grounding an analytic judgment on experience, because in forming such a judgment, I need not go out of the sphere of my concepts, and therefore recourse to the testimony of experience is quite unnecessary. That "bodies are extended" is not an empirical judgment, but a proposition that stands firm a priori. For before addressing myself to experience, I already have in my concept all the requisite conditions for the judgment, and I need only to extract the predicate from the concept, according to the principle of contradiction, and thereby at the same time become conscious of the necessity of the judgment—a necessity that I could never learn from experience. On the other hand, though at first I do not at all include the predicate of weight in my concept of body in general, that concept still indicates an object of experience, a part of the totality of experience, to which I can still add other parts; and this I do when I recognize by observation that bodies are heavy. I can know beforehand by analysis the concept of body through the characteristics of extension, impenetrability, shape, and so on, all which are thought in this concept. But now I extend my knowledge, and looking back on experience from which I had derived this concept of body, I find weight at all times connected with the above characteristics, and therefore I synthetically add to my concepts this as a predicate, and say "All bodies are heavy." Thus it is experience upon which rests the possibility of the synthesis of the predicate of weight with the concept of body, because both concepts, although the one is not contained in the other, still belong to one another (only contingently, however), as parts of a whole, namely, of experience, which is itself a synthesis of intuitions.

But to synthetic a priori judgments, such aid is entirely lacking. If I go out of and beyond the concept A, in order to recognize another B as connected with it, what foundation have I to rest on, whereby to render the synthesis possible? I have here no longer the advantage of looking out in the sphere of experience for what I want. Let us take, for example, the proposition "Everything that happens has a cause." In the concept of "something that happens," I indeed think an existence that is preceded by a certain time, and so on, and from this I can derive analytic judgments. But the concept of a cause lies quite out of the above concept and indicates something entirely different from "that which happens," and is consequently not contained in that concept. How then am I able to assert concerning the general concept "that which happens," something entirely different from that concept, and to recognize that the concept of cause, although not contained in it, yet belongs to it, and even necessarily? What is here the unknown = X, upon which the understanding rests when it believes it has found, out of the concept A, a foreign predicate B, which it nevertheless considers to be connected with it? It cannot be experience, because the principle adduced annexes the two representations, cause and effect, to [a third] representation, existence—not only with universality, which experience cannot give, but also with the expression of necessity—[something done] therefore completely a priori and from pure concepts. Upon such synthetic, that is, augmentative propositions, depends the whole aim of our speculative a priori knowledge; for although analytic judgments are indeed highly important and necessary, they are important and necessary only to arrive at that clearness of concepts that is requisite for a sure and extended synthesis, and this alone is a real acquisition.

### V. In All Theoretical Sciences of Reason, Synthetic A Priori Judgments Are Contained as Principles

1. Mathematical judgments are always synthetic. Up until now, this fact, though incontestably true and very important in its consequences, seems to have escaped the analysts of the human mind—in fact, to be in complete opposition to all their conjectures. For as it was found that mathematical conclusions all proceed according to the principle of contradiction (which the nature of every apodictic certainty[7] requires), people became persuaded that the fundamental principles of this science also were recognized and admitted in the same way. But the notion is fallacious; for although a synthetic proposition can certainly be discerned by means of the principle of contradiction, this is possible only when another synthetic proposition precedes, from which the latter is deduced, but never of itself.

Before all, it should be observed that proper mathematical propositions are always a priori judgments, and not empirical, because they carry along with them the concept of necessity, which cannot be given by experience. If this be objected, it does not matter; I will then limit my assertion to *pure* mathematics, the very concept of which implies that it consists of knowledge altogether nonempirical and a priori.

We might, indeed, at first suppose that the proposition $7 + 5 = 12$ is a merely analytic proposition, following (according to the principle of contradiction) from the concept of a sum of seven and five. But if we regard it more narrowly, we find that our concept of the sum of seven and five contains nothing more than the uniting of both sums into one, whereby it cannot at all be thought what this single number is that embraces both. The concept of twelve is by no means obtained by merely thinking the union of seven and five; and we may analyze our concept of such a possible sum as long as we wish, still we shall never discover in it the notion of twelve. We must go beyond these concepts and have recourse to an intuition that corresponds to one of the two—our five fingers, for example, or, like Segner in his *Arithmetic,*[8] five points—and so by degrees, add the units contained in the five given in the intuition, to the concept of seven. For I first take the number 7, and for the concept of 5 I call in the aid of the fingers of my hand as objects of intuition. I then add to the number 7 the units that I before took together (by means of the material image my hand) to make up the number 5, and by this process, I see the number 12 arise. That 7 should be added to 5, I have certainly thought in my concept of a sum = 7 + 5, but not that this sum was equal to 12. Arithmetical propositions are therefore always synthetic, of which we may become more clearly convinced by trying large numbers. For it will thus become quite evident that, turn and twist our concepts as we may, it is impossible, without having recourse to intuition, to arrive at the sum total or product by means of the mere analysis of our concepts. Just as little is any principle of pure geometry analytic. "A straight line between two points is the shortest" is a synthetic proposition. For my concept of *straight* contains no notion of *quantity,* but is merely *qualitative.* The concept of the *shortest* is therefore wholly an addition, and by no analysis can it be extracted from our concept of a straight line. Intuition must therefore here lend its aid, by means of which and thus only, our synthesis is possible. . . .

2. The science of natural philosophy (physics) contains in itself synthetic a priori judgments, as principles. I shall adduce two propositions: "In all changes of the material world, the quantity of matter remains unchanged" and "In all communication of motion, action and reaction must always be equal." In both of these, not only is the necessity—and therefore their a priori origin—clear, but also that they are synthetic propositions. For in the concept of matter, I do not think its permanency, but merely its presence in space, which it fills. I therefore really go out of and beyond the concept of matter in order to add to it something a priori, which I did not think in it. The proposition is therefore not analytic but synthetic, and nevertheless conceived a priori; and so it is with regard to the other propositions of the pure part of natural philosophy.

3. As to metaphysics, even if we look upon it merely as an attempted science—yet, from the nature of human reason, an indispensable one—we find that it must contain synthetic a priori propositions. It is not merely the duty of metaphysics to dissect, and thereby analytically to illustrate the concepts that we form a priori of things; but we seek to widen the range of our a priori knowledge. For this purpose, we must avail ourselves of principles that add something to the original concept—something not identical with, nor contained in it—and by means of synthetic a priori judgments, leave far behind us the limits of experience; for example, in the proposition

"The world must have a beginning," and such like. Thus metaphysics, according to the proper aim of the science, consists merely of synthetic a priori propositions.

## VI. The Universal Problem of Pure Reason

It is extremely advantageous to be able to bring a number of investigations under the formula of a single problem. For in this manner, we not only facilitate our own labor, inasmuch as we define it clearly to ourselves, but also render it easier for others to decide whether we have done justice to our undertaking. The proper problem of pure reason, then, is contained in the question "How are synthetic a priori judgments possible?"

That metaphysical science has until now remained in so vacillating a state of uncertainty and contradiction is only to be attributed to the fact that this great problem, and perhaps even the difference between analytic and synthetic judgments, did not sooner suggest itself to philosophers. Upon the solution of this problem, or upon sufficient proof of the impossibility of synthetic a priori knowledge, depends the existence or downfall of the science of metaphysics. Among philosophers, David Hume came the nearest of all to this problem; yet it never acquired in his mind sufficient precision, nor did he regard the question in its universality. On the contrary, he stopped short at the synthetic proposition of the connection of an effect with its cause *(principium causalitatis),*[9] insisting that such an a priori proposition was impossible. According to his conclusions, then, all that we term metaphysical science is a mere delusion, arising from the fancied insight of reason into that which is in truth borrowed from experience, and to which habit has given the appearance of necessity. Against this assertion, destructive to all pure philosophy, he would have been guarded, had he had our problem before his eyes in its universality. For he would then have perceived that, according to his own argument, there likewise could not be any pure mathematical science, which assuredly cannot exist without synthetic a priori propositions—an absurdity from which his good understanding must have saved him.

In the solution of the above problem is at the same time comprehended the possibility of the use of pure reason in the foundation and construction of all sciences that contain theoretical a priori knowledge of objects—that is to say, the answer to the following questions:

How is pure mathematical science possible?
How is pure natural science possible?

With respect to these sciences, since they do certainly exist, it may with propriety be asked how they are possible; for that they must be possible, is shown by the fact that they really exist. But as to metaphysics, the miserable progress it has made so far, and the fact that of no one system yet brought forward can be said, with regard to its true aim, to exist—these facts leave anyone at liberty to doubt with reason the very possibility of its existence.

Yet, in a certain sense, this kind of knowledge must unquestionably be looked upon as *given;* in other words, metaphysics must be considered as really existing, if not as a science, nevertheless as a natural disposition of the human mind *(metaphysica naturalis).*[10] For human reason, without any instigations imputable to the mere vanity of great knowledge, unceasingly progresses, urged on by its own feeling of need, towards such questions as cannot be answered by any empirical application of reason, or principles derived from it; and so there has always really existed in every man some system of metaphysics. It will always exist, so soon as reason awakes to the exercise of its power of speculation. And now the question arises: How is metaphysics, as a natural disposition, possible? In other words, how, from the nature of universal human reason, do those questions arise that pure reason proposes to itself and that it is impelled by its own feeling of need to answer as well as it can?

But since in all the attempts previously made to answer the questions that reason is prompted by its very nature to propose to itself—for example, whether the world had a beginning, or has existed from eternity—reason has always met with unavoidable contradictions, we must not rest satisfied with the mere natural disposition of the mind to metaphysics, that is, with the existence of the faculty of pure reason, from which, indeed, some sort of metaphysical system always arises. But it must be possible to arrive at certainty in regard to the question whether we know or do not know the things of which metaphysics treats. We must be able to arrive at a decision on the subjects of its questions, or on the ability or inability of reason to form any judgment respecting them; and therefore either to extend with confidence the bounds of our pure reason, or to set strictly defined and safe limits to its action. This last question that arises out of the above universal problem, would properly run thus: How is metaphysics possible as a science?

Thus, the critique of reason leads at last, naturally and necessarily, to science; and, on the other hand, the dogmatic use of reason without criticism leads to groundless assertions, against which others equally specious can always be set, thus ending unavoidably in skepticism.

Besides, this science cannot be of great and formidable prolixity, because it has not to do with objects of reason, the variety of which is inexhaustible, but merely with reason itself and its problems—problems that arise out of its own bosom, and are not proposed to it by the nature of outward things, but by its own nature. And when once reason has previously become able completely to understand its own power in regard to objects that it meets within experience, it will be easy to determine securely the extent and limits of its attempted application to objects beyond the confines of experience. . . .

### Transcendental Doctrine of Elements.[11] First Part: The Transcendental Aesthetic[12]

In whatever mode or by whatever means our knowledge may relate to objects, it is at least quite clear that the only manner in which it immediately relates to them, is by means of an *intuition*. To this as the indispensable groundwork, all thought points. But an intuition can take place only insofar as the object is given to us. This is only possible, to man at least, on the condition that the object affects the mind in a certain manner. The capacity for receiving representations (receptivity) through the mode in which we are affected by objects, is called *sensibility*. By means of sensibility, therefore, objects are given to us, and it alone furnishes us with intuitions. By the understanding they are *thought,* and from the understanding arise *concepts*. But all thought must, directly or indirectly, by means of certain signs, relate ultimately to intuitions, and consequently, with us, to sensibility, because in no other way can an object be given to us. . . .

The science of all the principles of sensibility a priori, I call transcendental aesthetic. There must, then, be such a science, forming the first part of the transcendental doctrine of elements, in distinction to the part that contains the principles of pure thought, which is called transcendental logic. . . .

### Section I. On Space

By means of the external sense (a property of the mind), we represent to ourselves objects as outside, and these all in space. In space alone are their shape, dimensions, and relations to each other determined or determinable. The internal sense, by means of which the mind contemplates itself or its internal state, gives, indeed, no intuition of the soul as an object; yet there is nevertheless a determinate form, under which alone the contemplation of our internal state is possible, so that all that which relates to the inward determinations of the mind is represented in relations of time. Of time we cannot have any external intuition, any more than we can have an internal intuition of space. What then are time and space? Are they real existences? Or are they merely relations or determinations of things, such, however, as would equally belong to these things in themselves, though they should never become objects of intuition? Or are they such as belong only to the form of intuition, and consequently to the subjective constitution of the mind, without which these predicates of time and space could not be attached to any object? In order to become informed on these points, we shall first give an exposition of the concept of space. By exposition, I mean the clear, though not detailed, representation of that which belongs to a concept; and an exposition is metaphysical when it contains that which represents the concept as given a priori.

1. Space is not a concept that has been derived from outward experiences. For, in order that certain sensations may relate to something outside me (that is, to something that occupies a different part of space from that in which I am), thus in order that I may represent them not merely as outside of and near to each other, but also in separate places, the representation of space must already exist as a foundation. Consequently, the representation of space cannot be borrowed from the relations of external phenomena through experience; but, on the contrary, this external experience is itself only possible through the antecedent representation.

2. Space then is a necessary representation a priori, which serves for the foundation of all external intuitions. We never can imagine or make a representation to ourselves of the nonexistence of space, though we may easily enough think that no objects are found in it. It must therefore be considered as the condition of the possibility of phenomena, and by no means as a determination dependent on them, and is a representation a priori, which necessarily supplies the basis for external phenomena. . . .

### Section II. On Time

1. Time is not an empirical concept. For neither coexistence nor succession would be perceived by us, if the representation of time did not exist as a foundation a priori. Without this presupposition we could not represent to ourselves that things exist together at one and the same time, or at different times—that is, contemporaneously, or in succession.

2. Time is a necessary representation, lying at the foundation of all our intuitions. With regard to phenomena in general, we cannot think away time from them, and represent them to ourselves as out of and unconnected with time, but we can quite well represent to ourselves time void of phenomena. Time is therefore given a priori. In it alone all reality of phenomena is possible. These may all be annihilated in thought, but time itself, as the universal condition of their possibility, cannot be so annulled. . . .

### Analytic of Concepts. Chapter 1: On the Transcendental Clue to the Discovery of All Pure Concepts of the Understanding

### Section II. Of the Logical Function of the Understanding in Judgments

If we abstract all the content of a judgment, and consider only the intellectual form of it, we find that the function of thought in a judgment can be brought under four heads, of which each contains three moments. These may be conveniently represented in the following table:

I.

*Quantity of Judgments*

Universal

Particular

Singular

II.

*Quality*

Affirmative

Negative

Infinite

III.

*Relation*

Categorical

Hypothetical

Disjunctive

IV.

*Modality*

Problematic

Assertoric

Apodictic . . .

### Section III. Of the Pure Concepts of the Understanding, or Categories

. . . There arise exactly so many pure concepts of the understanding, applying a priori to objects of intuition in general, as there are logical functions in all possible judgments. For there is no other function or faculty existing in the understanding besides those enumerated in that table. These concepts we shall, with Aristotle, call categories,[13] our purpose being originally identical with his, notwithstanding the great difference in the execution.

Table of Categories

I.

*Of Quantity*

Unity

Plurality

Totality

II.

*Of Quality*

Reality

Negation

Limitation

III.

*Of Relation*

Of Inherence and Subsistence
(*substantia et accidens*)[14]

Of Causality and Dependence
(cause and effect)

Of Community
(reciprocity between agent and patient)[15]

IV.

*Of Modality*

Prossibility—Impossibility

Existence—Nonexistence

Necessity—Contingency . . .

This, then, is a catalog of all the originally pure concepts of the synthesis that the understanding contains a priori, and these concepts alone entitle it to be called a pure understanding, inasmuch as only by them it can render the manifold of intuition conceivable—in other words, think an object of intuition. This division is made systematically from a common principle—namely, the faculty of judgment (which is just the same as the power of thought)—and has not arisen rhapsodically from a haphazard search for pure concepts, the full number of which we could never be certain, since we would employ induction alone and would not consider that, by this method, we could never understand why precisely these concepts, and no others, abide in the pure understanding.

---

► NOTES

1. *metaphysical:* relating to *metaphysics,* the branch of philosophy that studies the fundamental nature of reality [D. C. ABEL, EDITOR]

2. *a priori:* independent of experience (literally, in Latin, "from what comes earlier"); contrasted with *a posteriori,* dependent on experience ("from what comes later") [D. C. ABEL]

3. Nicolaus Copernicus (1473–1543) was a Polish astronomer. [D. C. ABEL]

4. *intuition:* sense experience [D. C. ABEL]

5. *contingency:* the state of being able to be or not to be; contrasted with *necessity* [D. C. ABEL]

6. David Hume (1711–1776) was a Scottish philosopher and historian. [D. C. ABEL]

7. *apodictic certainty:* absolute certainty [D. C. ABEL]

8. Johann Andreas von Segner, *Anfangsgründe der Arithmetic, Geometrie and der Geometrischen Berechnungen* (1756). Segner (1704–1777) was a German mathematician and naturalist. [D. C. ABEL]

9. *principium causalitatis:* (Latin) the principle of causality [D. C. ABEL]

10. *metaphysica naturalis:* (Latin) natural metaphysics [D. C. ABEL]

11. *Transcendental Doctrine of Elements: Elements* are the forms that our minds impose on objects; the doctrine Kant proposes is *transcendental* because the forms that our minds impose are a priori and thus transcend the objects themselves. [D. C. ABEL]

12. *Aesthetic:* something pertaining to sensation (*aisthēsis* in Greek) [D. C. ABEL]

13. The Greek philosopher Aristotle (384–322 B.C.E.) wrote a treatise called *Categories* (*Katēgoriai,* "predicates"), which postulates ten ways in which we think about things and in which things exist. [D. C. ABEL]

14. *substantia et accidens:* (Latin) substance [what subsists in itself] and accident [what inheres in a substance] [D. C. ABEL]

15. *agent and patient:* that which acts, and that which is acted upon [D. C. ABEL]

# Critique of Pure Reason

Immanuel Kant

Immanuel Kant was born in 1724 in Königsberg, Prussia, where he spent his entire life. As a boy he attended the Collegium Fridericanum, a school run by the Pietists (the Lutheran sect to which his family belonged). In 1740 he enrolled in the University of Königsberg, where he studied a wide variety of subjects, including theology, philosophy, mathematics, physics, and medicine. He withdrew from the university in 1747 to support himself by working as a private tutor for families in the Königsberg area. He resumed his studies in 1754 and completed his degree the following year. He then became a lecturer at the University of Königsberg, teaching such diverse subjects as mathematics, geography, mineralogy, and philosophy. Fifteen years later he was appointed Professor of Logic and Metaphysics. His writings—especially his monumental *Critique of Pure Reason* (1781)—brought him increasing fame, and students came from afar to hear him lecture. In 1797 he stopped lecturing, but he continued to write. He died in Königsberg in 1804 at the age of seventy-nine.

Kant's principal works, in addition to the *Critique of Pure Reason,* are *Prolegomena to Any Future Metaphysics* (1783), *Fundamental Principles of the Metaphysics of Morals* (1785), *Critique of Practical Reason* (1788), *Critique of Judgment* (1790), and *The Metaphysics of Morals* (1797).

Our reading is from the section of the *Critique of Pure Reason* entitled "Of the Impossibility of an Ontological Proof of the Existence of God." An "ontological" proof of God's existence is one based solely on the concept or meaning of the term "God." According to this kind of proof, to deny that God exists is to contradict oneself. "God" means "an all-perfect being," and since existence is a perfection, God necessarily exists. For if God did *not* exist, God would lack a perfection and thus not be an all-perfect being—an obvious contradiction of the original concept of God. Just as we can deduce from the concept of triangle that a triangle has three angles, so we can deduce from the concept of God that God exists.

Kant rejects the ontological approach to proving God's existence. He argues that necessity applies to *judgments,* not to *things.* While it *is* contradictory to suppose that a triangle exists and to judge that it does not have three angles, it is *not* contradictory to suppose that neither a triangle nor angles exist. Similarly, there is no contradiction in supposing that neither God nor God's perfections exist. Moreover, Kant denies that existence is part of our concept of God, or of any other being. For example, my concept of a hundred dollars is the same as my concept of a hundred *existing* dollars. To say that something exists is to affirm that there is an *object corresponding to* our concept. It is therefore a mistake to deduce from our concept of God that there is an object corresponding to our concept.

▼

**Part I, Transcendental Doctrine of Elements; Second Part, Transcendental Logic; Second Division, Transcendental Dialectic**

**Chapter III, The Ideal of Pure Reason; Section 4, Of the Impossibility of an Ontological Proof of the Existence of God** . . . Philosophers have always talked of an *absolutely necessary* being and have nevertheless declined to take the trouble of conceiving whether—and how—a being of this nature is even cogitable, not to mention that its existence is actually demonstrable.

A verbal definition of the conception is certainly easy enough; it is something, the nonexistence of which is impossible. But does this definition throw any light upon the conditions which render it impossible to cogitate the nonexistence of a thing—conditions which we wish to ascertain, that we may discover whether we think anything in the conception of such a being or not? For the mere fact that I throw away, by means of the word "unconditioned," all the conditions which the understanding habitually requires in order to regard anything as necessary, is very far from making clear whether by means of the conception of the unconditionally necessary I think of something, or really of nothing at all.

Nay, more, this chance-conception, now become so current, many have endeavored to explain by examples which seemed to render any inquiries regarding its intelligibility quite needless. Every geometrical proposition—for example, that a triangle has three angles—it was said, is absolutely necessary; and thus people talked of an object which lay out of the sphere of our understanding as if it were perfectly plain what the conception of such a being meant.

All the examples adduced have been drawn, without exception, from *judgments* and not from *things*. But the unconditioned necessity of a judgment does not form the absolute necessity of a thing. On the contrary, the absolute necessity of a judgment is only a conditioned necessity of a thing, or of the predicate in a judgment. The proposition above-mentioned does not [declare] that three angles necessarily exist, but that, upon condition that a triangle exists, three angles must necessarily exist in it. And thus this logical necessity has been the source of the greatest delusions. Having formed an a priori[1] conception of a thing, the content of which was made to embrace existence, we believed ourselves safe in concluding that, because existence belongs necessarily to the object of the conception (that is, under the condition of my positing this thing as given), the existence of the thing is also posited necessarily, and that it is therefore absolutely necessary—merely because its existence has been cogitated in the conception.

If, in an identical judgment, I annihilate the predicate in thought and retain the subject, a contradiction is the result; and hence I say, the former belongs necessarily to the latter. But if I suppress both subject *and* predicate in thought, no contradiction arises; for there *is nothing* at all, and therefore no means of forming a contradiction. To suppose the existence of a triangle and not that of its three angles, is self-contradictory; but to suppose the nonexistence of both triangle and angles is perfectly admissible. And so is it with the conception of an absolutely necessary being. Annihilate its existence in thought, and you annihilate the thing itself with all its predicates. How then can there be any room for contradiction? Externally, there is nothing to give rise to a contradiction, for a thing cannot be necessary externally; nor internally, for, by the annihilation or suppression of the thing itself, its internal properties are also annihilated. God is omnipotent—that is a necessary judgment. His omnipotence cannot be denied, if the existence of a Deity is posited—the existence, that is, of an infinite being, the two conceptions being identical. But when you say "God does not exist," neither omnipotence nor any other predicate is affirmed; they must all disappear with the subject, and in this judgment there cannot exist the least self-contradiction.

You have thus seen that when the predicate of a judgment is annihilated in thought along with the subject, no internal contradiction can arise, be the predicate what it may. There is no possibility of evading the conclusion; you find yourselves compelled to declare: There are certain subjects which cannot be annihilated in thought. But this is nothing more than saying: There exist subjects which are absolutely necessary—the very hypothesis which you are called upon to establish. For I find myself unable to form the slightest conception of a thing which, when annihilated in thought with all its predicates, leaves behind a contradiction; and contradiction is the only criterion of impossibility, in the sphere of pure a priori conceptions.

Against these general considerations, the justice of which no one can dispute, one argument is adduced which is regarded as furnishing a satisfactory demonstration from fact. It is affirmed that there is one and only one conception in which the nonbeing or annihilation of the object is self-contradictory, and this is the conception of an *ens realissimum*.[2] It possesses, you say, all reality, and you feel yourself justified in admitting the possibility of such a being. (This I am willing to grant for the present, although the existence of a conception which is not self-contradictory, is far from being sufficient to prove the possibility of an object.)[3] Now the notion of all reality embraces in it that of existence; the notion of existence lies, therefore, in the conception of this possible thing. If this thing is annihilated in thought, the internal possibility of the thing is also annihilated, which is self-contradictory.

I answer: It is absurd to introduce (under whatever term disguised) into the conception of a thing, which is to be cogitated solely in reference to its possibility, the conception of its existence. If this is admitted, you will have apparently gained the day, but in reality have [stated] nothing but a mere tautology.[4] I ask, is the proposition "This or that thing (which I am admitting to be possible) exists" an analytic or a synthetic proposition?[5] If the former, there is no addition made to the subject of your thought by the affirmation of its existence; but then the conception in your minds is identical with the thing itself, or you have supposed the existence of a thing to be possible, and then inferred its existence from its internal possibility—which is but a miserable tautology. The word "reality" in the conception of the thing, and the word "existence" in the conception of the predicate, will not help you out of the difficulty. For, supposing you were to term all positing of a thing "reality," you have thereby posited the thing with all its predicates in the conception of the subject and assumed its actual existence, and this you merely repeat in the predicate. But if you confess, as every reasonable person must, that every existential proposition is synthetic, how can it be maintained that the predicate of existence cannot be denied without contradiction—a property which is the characteristic of analytic propositions alone?

I should have a reasonable hope of putting an end forever to this sophistical mode of argumentation, by a strict definition of the conception of existence, did not my own experience teach me that the illusion arising from our confounding a logical with a real predicate (a predicate which aids in the determination of a thing) resists almost all the endeavors of explanation and illustration. A *logical predicate* may be what you please; even the subject may be predicated of itself—for logic pays no regard to the content of a judgment. But [a *determining predicate*] is a predicate which adds to and enlarges the conception. It must not, therefore, be contained in the conception.

"Being" is evidently not a real predicate, that is, a conception of something which is added to the conception of some other thing. It is merely the positing of a thing, or of certain determinations in it. Logically, it is merely the copula[6] of a judgment. The proposition "God is omnipotent" contains two conceptions, which have a certain object or content; the word "is" is no additional predicate—it merely indicates the relation of the predicate to the subject. Now if I take the subject (God) with all its predicates (omnipotence being one) and say "God is" or "There is a God," I add no new predicate to the conception of God; I merely posit or affirm the existence of the subject with all its predicates—I posit the *object* in relation to my *conception*. The content of both is the same; and there is no addition made to the conception (which expresses merely the possibility of the object) by my cogitating the object (in the expression "it *is*") as absolutely given or existing. Thus the real contains no more than the possible. A hundred real dollars contain no more than a hundred possible dollars. For, as the latter indicate the conception, and the former the object, on the supposition that the content of the former was greater than that of the latter, my conception would not be an expression of the whole object and would consequently be an inadequate conception of it. But in reckoning my wealth there may be said to be more in a hundred real dollars than in a hundred possible dollars—that is, in the mere conception of them. For the real object (the dollars) is not analytically contained in my conception, but forms a synthetic addition to my conception (which is merely a determination of my mental state), although this objective reality (this existence) outside my conception does not in the least degree increase the [conceived] hundred dollars.

By whatever and by whatever *number* of predicates—even to the complete determination of it—I may cogitate a thing, I do not in the least augment the object of my conception by the addition of the statement "this thing exists." Otherwise, not exactly the same, but something more than what was cogitated in my conception, would exist, and I could not affirm

Abel
Discourses

Philosophy of Religion

Immanuel Kant
Critique of Pure Reason
(selection 2)

© McGraw–Hill, Inc., 1995

that the exact object of my conception had real existence. If I cogitate a thing as containing all modes of reality except one, the mode of reality which is absent is not added to the conception of the thing by the affirmation that the thing exists; on the contrary, the thing exists (if it exists at all) with the same defect as that cogitated in its conception; otherwise not that which was cogitated, but something different, exists. Now if I cogitate a being as the highest reality, without defect or imperfection, the question still remains whether this being exists or not. For although no element is wanting in the possible real content of my conception, there is a defect in its relation to my mental state—that is, I am ignorant whether cognition of the object indicated by the conception is also possible a posteriori.[7] And here the cause of the present difficulty becomes apparent. If the question regarded an object of sense merely, it would be impossible for me to confound the conception with the existence of a thing. For the conception merely enables me to cogitate an object as according with the general conditions of experience; while the *existence* of the object permits me to cogitate it as contained in the sphere of actual experience. At the same time, this connection with the world of experience does not in the least augment the conception, although a possible perception has been added to the experience of the mind. But if we cogitate existence by the pure category alone, it is not to be wondered at, that we should find ourselves unable to present any criterion sufficient to distinguish it from mere possibility.

Whatever be the content of our conception of an object, it is necessary to go beyond it if we wish to predicate existence of the object. In the case of sensuous objects,[8] this is attained by their connection according to empirical laws with some one of my perceptions; but there is no means of cognizing the existence of objects of pure thought, because it must be cognized completely a priori. But all our knowledge of existence (be it immediately by perception, or by inferences connecting some object with a perception) belongs entirely to the sphere of experience, which is in perfect unity with itself. And although an existence out of this sphere cannot be absolutely declared to be impossible, it is a hypothesis the truth of which we have no means of ascertaining.

The notion of a Supreme Being is in many respects a highly useful idea; but for the very reason that it is an idea, it is incapable of enlarging our cognition with regard to the existence of things. It is not even sufficient to instruct us as to the possibility of a being which we do not know to exist. The analytic criterion of possibility, which consists in the absence of contradiction in propositions, cannot be denied it. But the connection of real properties in a thing is a synthesis, the possibility of which an a priori judgment cannot be formed because these realities are not presented to us specifically. And even if this were to happen, a judgment would still be impossible because the criterion of the possibility of synthetic cognitions must be sought for in the world of experience, to which the object of an idea cannot belong. . . .

Abel
Discourses

Philosophy of Religion

Immanuel Kant
Critique of Pure Reason
(selection 2)

© McGraw–Hill, Inc., 1995

111

The celebrated ontological . . . argument for the existence of a Supreme Being is therefore insufficient, and we may as well hope to increase our stock of knowledge by the aid of mere ideas, as the merchant to augment his wealth by the addition of [zeros] to his cash account.

---

▶ NOTES

1. *a priori:* independent of experience (literally, in Latin, "from what comes earlier") [D.C.A., ed.]

2. *ens realissimum:* most real entity (Latin) [D.C.A.]

3. A conception is always possible if it is not self-contradictory. . . . But it may be, notwithstanding, an empty conception unless the objective reality of this synthesis, by which it is generated, is demonstrated; and a proof of this kind must be based on principles of possible experience, and not on the principle of analysis or contradiction. [I.K.]

4. *tautology:* a repetition of the same idea [D.C.A.]

5. An *analytic proposition* is one whose predicate is contained in the concept of the subject; a *synthetic proposition* is one whose predicate is not contained in the concept of the subject. [D.C.A.]

6. *copula:* a link between the subject and predicate of a proposition [D.C.A.]

7. *a posteriori:* dependent on experience; in experience (literally, in Latin, "from what comes later") [D.C.A.]

8. *sensuous objects:* objects that can be sensed [D.C.A.]

Abel
Discourses

Ethical Theories

Friedrich Nietzsche
Beyond Good and Evil
(selection)

© McGraw–Hill, Inc., 1994

# Beyond Good and Evil

Friedrich Nietzsche

Friedrich Nietzsche was born in Röcken, Prussia, in 1844. After graduating from the Lutheran boarding school at Pforta in 1864, he enrolled in the University of Bonn to study theology. There he began to doubt his Christian faith (he eventually became an atheist and harsh critic of Christianity) and in 1865 transferred to the University of Leipzig to study classical philology (Greek and Latin language and literature) and music. He was recognized as a brilliant student of philology, and at the age of twenty-four, before he had even finished his doctorate, he was offered the chair of classical philology at the University of Basel in Switzerland. The University of Leipzig quickly granted his degree, and Nietzsche assumed the professorship at Basel in 1869. Ten years later, because of his increasingly bad health, Nietzsche resigned his position. For the next ten years, half blind and in unremitting pain, he wandered through Switzerland, Germany, and Italy in search of a cure. His mental health began to deteriorate as well; in 1889 he collapsed on the streets of Turin, Italy, completely insane. He died in Weimar in 1900.

Nietzsche's principal works are *The Birth of Tragedy out of the Spirit of Music* (1872), *Human, All Too Human* (1878), *The Gay Science* (1882), *Thus Spoke Zarathustra* (1883–1885), *Beyond Good and Evil* (1886), and *On the Genealogy of Morals* (1887).

Our selection is from *Beyond Good and Evil,* a book consisting of about three hundred aphorisms on various subjects. The topic of Chapter 9, from which our reading comes, is "What Is Noble?" According to Nietzsche, to be noble means to see oneself as the center and origin of all value. In fact, the terms "good" and "bad" originally designated simply what the aristocracy did and did not value. For Nietzsche, "life *is* precisely the will to power," and historically members of the aristocracy exercised their will to power by exploiting common people and using them as they saw fit. Nietzsche calls the morality of the ruling aristocracy a "master morality." He contrasts this kind of morality with "slave morality," which arose when common people tried to make their inferior and despicable lives more bearable by exalting as virtues such qualities as kindness, sympathy, selflessness, patience, and humility (the cornerstones of Christian morality). Slave morality gave rise to the pair of terms "good" and "evil," which Nietzsche contrasts with the "good" and "bad" of master morality. In slave morality, "good" refers to the slaves' (false) values, and "evil" to the (legitimate and noble) values of the rulers. Since rulers are not in the inferior position of slaves, they need not subscribe to slave values and are "beyond good and evil."

Nietzsche bemoans the fact that modern civilization, with its democratic and egalitarian tendencies, is replacing life-affirming master morality with life-denying slave morality. Yet there are still elements of master morality in some souls, and it is to these souls that Nietzsche's praise of "what is noble" is addressed.

▼

## Chapter 9: What Is Noble?

**257** Every elevation of the type "man" has hitherto been the work of an aristocratic society—and so will it always be—a society believing in a long scale of gradations of rank and differences of worth among human beings, and requiring slavery in some form or other. Without the *pathos of distance,* such as grows out of the incarnated difference of classes, out of the constant outlooking and downlooking of the ruling caste on subordinates and

Abel
Discourses

Ethical Theories

Friedrich Nietzsche
Beyond Good and Evil
(selection)

© McGraw–Hill, Inc., 1994

113

instruments, and out of their equally constant practice of obeying and commanding, of keeping down and keeping at a distance—that other more mysterious pathos could never have arisen, the longing for an ever new widening of distance within the soul itself, the formation of ever higher, rarer, further, more extended, more comprehensive states—in short, just the elevation of the type "man," the continued "self-surmounting of man," to use a moral formula in a supermoral sense. To be sure, one must not resign oneself to any humanitarian illusions about the history of the origin of an aristocratic society (that is to say, of the preliminary condition for the elevation of the type "man"): the truth is hard. Let us acknowledge unprejudicedly how every higher civilisation hitherto has *originated!* Men with a still natural nature—barbarians in every terrible sense of the word, men of prey, still in possession of unbroken strength of will and desire for power—threw themselves upon weaker, more moral, more peaceful races (perhaps trading or cattle-rearing communities), or upon old mellow civilisations in which the final vital force was flickering out in brilliant fireworks of wit and depravity. At the commencement, the noble caste was always the barbarian caste. Their superiority did not consist first of all in their physical, but in their psychical power—they were more *complete* men (which at every point also implies the same as "more complete beasts").

**258** Corruption—as the indication that anarchy threatens to break out among the instincts, and that the foundation of the emotions, called "life," is convulsed—is something radically different according to the organisation in which it manifests itself. When, for instance, an aristocracy like that of France at the beginning of the Revolution flung away its privileges with sublime disgust and sacrificed itself to an excess of its moral sentiments, it was corruption—it was really only the closing act of the corruption which had existed for centuries, by virtue of which that aristocracy had abdicated step by step its lordly prerogatives and lowered itself to a *function* of royalty (in the end even to its decoration and parade-dress). The essential thing, however, in a good and healthy aristocracy is that it should *not* regard itself as a function either of the kingship or the commonwealth, but as the *significance* and highest justification [of it]—that it should therefore accept with a good conscience the sacrifice of a legion of individuals who, *for its sake,* must be suppressed and reduced to imperfect men, to slaves and instruments. Its fundamental belief must be precisely that society is *not* allowed to exist for its own sake, but only as a foundation and scaffolding by means of which a select class of beings may be able to elevate themselves to their higher duties, and in general to a higher e*xistence*—like those sun-seeking climbing plants in Java (they are called *Sipo matador*), which encircle an oak so long and so often with their arms, until at last, high above it, but supported by it, they can unfold their tops in the open light and exhibit their happiness.

114

**Abel**
**Discourses**

**Ethical Theories**

**Friedrich Nietzsche**
**Beyond Good and Evil**
**(selection)**

© McGraw–Hill, Inc., 1994

**259**  To refrain mutually from injury, from violence, from exploitation, and to put one's will on a par with that of others—this may result in a certain rough sense in good conduct among individuals when the necessary conditions are given (namely, the actual similarity of the individuals in amount of force and degree of worth, and their co-relation within one organisation). As soon, however, as one wished to take this principle more generally, and if possible even as *the fundamental principle of society,* it would immediately disclose what it really is—namely, a will to the *denial* of life, a principle of dissolution and decay. Here one must think profoundly to the very basis and resist all sentimental weakness: life itself is *essentially* appropriation, injury, conquest of the strange and weak, suppression, severity, obtrusion of peculiar forms, incorporation, and at the least (putting it most mildly), exploitation. But why should one forever use precisely these words on which for ages a disparaging purpose has been stamped? Even the organisation within which, as was previously supposed, the individuals treat each other as equal—it takes place in every healthy aristocracy—must itself, if it be a living and not a dying organisation, do all that towards other bodies, which the individuals within it refrain from doing to each other: it will have to be the incarnated will to power, it will endeavour to grow, to gain ground, attract to itself and acquire ascendency—not owing to any morality or immorality, but because it *lives,* and because life *is* precisely will to power. On no point, however, is the ordinary consciousness of Europeans more unwilling to be corrected than on this matter; people now rave everywhere, even under the guise of science, about coming conditions of society in which "the exploiting character" is to be absent. That sounds to my ears as if they promised to invent a mode of life which should refrain from all organic functions. "Exploitation" does not belong to a depraved, or imperfect and primitive society: it belongs to the *nature* of the living being as a primary organic function; it is a consequence of the intrinsic will to power, which is precisely the will to life. Granting that as a theory this is a novelty—as a reality it is the *fundamental fact* of all history: let us be so far honest towards ourselves!

**260**  In a tour through the many finer and coarser moralities which have hitherto prevailed or still prevail on the earth, I found certain traits recurring regularly together and connected with one another, until finally two primary types revealed themselves to me, and a radical distinction was brought to light. There is *master morality* and *slave morality*—I would at once add, however, that in all higher and mixed civilisations, there are also attempts at the reconciliation of the two moralities; but one finds still oftener the confusion and mutual misunderstanding of them, indeed, sometimes their close juxtaposition—even in the same man, within one soul. The distinctions of moral values have either originated in a ruling caste, pleasantly conscious of being different from the ruled—or among the ruled class, the

Abel
Discourses

Ethical Theories

Friedrich Nietzsche
Beyond Good and Evil
(selection)

© McGraw–Hill, Inc., 1994

115

slaves and dependents of all sorts. In the first case, when it is the rulers who determine the conception "good," it is the exalted, proud disposition which is regarded as the distinguishing feature, and that which determines the order of rank. The noble type of man separates from himself the beings in whom the opposite of this exalted, proud disposition displays itself: he despises them. Let it at once be noted that in this first kind of morality the antithesis "good" and "bad" means practically the same as "noble" and "despicable"—the antithesis "good" and "evil" is of a different origin. The cowardly, the timid, the insignificant, and those thinking merely of narrow utility are despised; also the distrustful, with their constrained glances, the self-abasing, the dog-like kind of men who let themselves be abused, the mendicant flatterers, and above all the liars—it is a fundamental belief of all aristocrats that the common people are untruthful. "We truthful ones" the nobility in ancient Greece called themselves. It is obvious that everywhere the designations of moral value were at first applied to *men* and were only derivatively and at a later period applied to *actions;* it is a gross mistake, therefore, when historians of morals start with questions like, "Why have sympathetic actions been praised?" The noble type of man regards *himself* as a determiner of values; he does not require to be approved of; he passes the judgment, "What is injurious to me is injurious in itself"; he knows that it is he himself only who confers honour on things; he is a *creator of values*. He honours whatever he recognises in himself: such morality is self-glorification. In the foreground there is the feeling of plenitude, of power, which seeks to overflow, the happiness of high tension, the consciousness of a wealth which would give and bestow. The noble man also helps the unfortunate, but not—or scarcely—out of pity, but rather from an impulse generated by the superabundance of power. The noble man honours in himself the powerful one, him also who has power over himself, who knows how to speak and how to keep silence, who takes pleasure in subjecting himself to severity and hardness, and has reverence for all that is severe and hard. "Wotan placed a hard heart in my breast," says an old Scandinavian saga: it is thus rightly expressed from the soul of a proud Viking. Such a type of man is even proud of *not* being made for sympathy; the hero of the saga therefore adds warningly: "He who has not a hard heart when young, will never have one." The noble and brave who think thus are the furthest removed from the morality which sees precisely in sympathy, or in acting for the good of others, or in *désintéressement,*[1] the characteristic of the moral; faith in oneself, pride in oneself, a radical enmity and irony towards "selflessness," belong as definitely to noble morality as do a careless scorn and precaution in presence of sympathy and the "warm heart." It is the powerful who *know* how to honour; it is their art, their domain for invention. The profound reverence for age and for tradition (all law rests on this double reverence), the belief and prejudice in favour of ancestors and unfavourable to newcomers, is typical in the morality of the powerful. And if, reversely, men of "modern ideas" believe almost

Abel                           Ethical Theories          Friedrich Nietzsche        © McGraw–Hill, Inc., 1994
Discourses                                                Beyond Good and Evil
                                                          (selection)

instinctively in "progress" and the "future" and are more and more lacking in respect for old age, the ignoble origin of these "ideas" has complacently betrayed itself thereby. A morality of the ruling class, however, is more especially foreign and irritating to present-day taste in the sternness of its principle that one has duties only to one's equals, that one may act towards beings of a lower rank, towards all that is foreign, just as seems good to one, or "as the heart desires," and in any case "beyond good and evil." It is here that sympathy and similar sentiments can have a place. The ability and obligation to exercise prolonged gratitude and prolonged revenge (both only within the circle of equals), artfulness in retaliation, *raffinement*[2] of the idea in friendship, a certain necessity to have enemies (as outlets for the emotions of envy, quarrelsomeness, arrogance—in fact, in order to be a good *friend*): all these are typical characteristics of the noble morality, which, as has been pointed out, is not the morality of "modern ideas" and is therefore at present difficult to realise, and also to unearth and disclose. It is otherwise with the second type of morality, *slave morality*. Supposing that the abused, the oppressed, the suffering, the unemancipated, the weary, and those uncertain of themselves, should moralise; what will be the common element in their moral estimates? Probably a pessimistic suspicion with regard to the entire situation of man will find expression, perhaps a condemnation of man, together with his situation. The slave has an unfavourable eye for the virtues of the powerful; he has a scepticism and distrust, a refinement of distrust of everything "good" that is there honoured—he would persuade himself that the very happiness there is not genuine. On the other hand, those qualities which serve to alleviate the existence of sufferers are brought into prominence and flooded with light; it is here that sympathy, the kind, helping hand, the warm heart, patience, diligence, humility, and friendliness attain to honour; for here these are the most useful qualities and almost the only means of supporting the burden of existence. Slave morality is essentially the morality of utility. Here is the seat of the origin of the famous antithesis "good" and *"evil"*—power and dangerousness are assumed to reside in the evil, a certain dreadfulness, subtlety, and strength, which do not admit of being despised. According to slave morality, therefore, the "evil" man arouses fear; according to master morality, it is precisely the "good" man who arouses fear and seeks to arouse it, while the bad man is regarded as the despicable being. The contrast attains its maximum when, in accordance with the logical consequences of slave morality, a shade of depreciation—it may be slight and well-intentioned—at last attaches itself even to the "good" man of this morality; because, according to the servile mode of thought, the good man must in any case be the *safe* man: he is good-natured, easily deceived, perhaps a little stupid, *un bonhomme.*[3] Everywhere that slave morality gains the ascendency, language shows a tendency to approximate the significations of the words "good" and "stupid." A last fundamental difference: the desire for *freedom,* the instinct for happiness and the refinements of the feeling of

Abel
Discourses

Ethical Theories

Friedrich Nietzsche
Beyond Good and Evil
(selection)

© McGraw–Hill, Inc., 1994

117

liberty belong as necessarily to slave morals and morality, as artifice and enthusiasm in reverence and devotion are the regular symptoms of an aristocratic mode of thinking and estimating. Hence we can understand without further detail why love *as a passion*—it is our European speciality—must absolutely be of noble origin. As is well known, its invention is due to the Provençal poet-cavaliers, those brilliant ingenious men of the *"gai saber,"*[4] to whom Europe owes so much, and almost owes itself.

**261** Vanity is one of the things which are perhaps most difficult for a noble man to understand: he will be tempted to deny it, where another kind of man thinks he sees it self-evidently. The problem for him is to represent to his mind beings who seek to arouse a good opinion of themselves which they themselves do not possess—and consequently also do not "deserve"—and who yet *believe* in this good opinion afterwards. This seems to him on the one hand such bad taste and so self-disrespectful, and on the other hand so grotesquely unreasonable, that he would like to consider vanity an exception and is doubtful about it in most cases when it is spoken of. He will say, for instance: "I may be mistaken about my value, and on the other hand may nevertheless demand that my value should be acknowledged by others precisely as I rate it—that, however, is not vanity (but self-conceit, or, in most cases, that which is called 'humility,' and also 'modesty')." Or he will even say: "For many reasons I can delight in the good opinion of others, perhaps because I love and honour them and rejoice in all their joys, perhaps also because their good opinion endorses and strengthens my belief in my own good opinion, perhaps because the good opinion of others, even in cases where I do not share it, is useful to me, or gives promise of usefulness—all this, however, is not vanity." The man of noble character must first bring it home forcibly to his mind, especially with the aid of history, that, from time immemorial, in all social strata in any way dependent, the ordinary man *was* only that which he *passed for*; not being at all accustomed to fix values, he did not assign even to himself any other value than that which his master assigned to him (it is the peculiar *right of masters* to create values). It may be looked upon as the result of an extraordinary atavism[5] that the ordinary man, even at present, is still always *waiting* for an opinion about himself, and then instinctively submitting himself to it; yet by no means only to a "good" opinion, but also to a bad and unjust one (think, for instance, of the greater part of the self-appreciations and self-depreciations which believing women learn from their confessors, and which in general the believing Christian learns from his church). In fact, conformably to the slow rise of the democratic social order (and its cause, the blending of the blood of masters and slaves), the originally noble and rare impulse of the masters to assign a value to themselves and to "think well" of themselves will now be more and more encouraged and extended. But it has at all times an older, ampler, and more radi-

118

Abel
Discourses

Ethical Theories

Friedrich Nietzsche
Beyond Good and Evil
(selection)

© McGraw–Hill, Inc., 1994

cally ingrained propensity opposed to it—and in the phenomenon of "vanity" this older propensity overmasters the younger. The vain person rejoices over *every* good opinion which he hears about himself (quite apart from the point of view of its usefulness, and equally regardless of its truth or falsehood), just as he suffers from every bad opinion: for he subjects himself to both, he *feels* himself subjected to both, by that oldest instinct of subjection which breaks forth in him. It is "the slave" in the vain man's blood, the remains of the slave's craftiness—and how much of the "slave" is still left in woman, for instance!—which seeks to *seduce* to good opinions of itself; it is the slave, too, who immediately afterwards falls prostrate himself before these opinions, as though he had not called them forth. And to repeat it again: vanity is an atavism. . . .

**265**  At the risk of displeasing innocent ears, I submit that egoism belongs to the essence of a noble soul—I mean the unalterable belief that to a being such as "we," other beings must naturally be in subjection, and have to sacrifice themselves. The noble soul accepts the fact of his egoism without question, and also without consciousness of harshness, constraint, or arbitrariness therein, but rather as something that may have its basis in the primary law of things. If he sought a designation for it, he would say: "It is justice itself." He acknowledges under certain circumstances, which made him hesitate at first, that there are other equally privileged ones; as soon as he has settled this question of rank, he moves among those equals and equally privileged ones with the same assurance, as regards modesty and delicate respect, which he enjoys in intercourse with himself—in accordance with an innate heavenly mechanism which all the stars understand. It is an *additional* instance of his egoism, this artfulness and self-limitation in intercourse with his equals (every star is a similar egoist). He honours *himself* in them; and in the rights which he concedes to them, he has no doubt that the exchange of honours and rights, as the *essence* of all intercourse, belongs also to the natural condition of things. The noble soul gives as he takes, prompted by the passionate and sensitive instinct of requital, which is at the root of his nature. The notion of "favour" has, *inter pares,*[6] neither significance nor good repute; there may be a sublime way of letting gifts, as it were, light upon one from above, and of drinking them thirstily like dewdrops; but for those arts and displays the noble soul has no aptitude. His egoism hinders him here: in general, he looks "aloft" unwillingly—he looks either *forward,* horizontally and deliberately, or downwards; *he knows that he is on a height.* . . .

**272**  Signs of nobility: never to think of lowering our duties to the rank of duties for everybody; to be unwilling to renounce or to share our responsibilities; to count our prerogatives, and the exercise of them, among our *duties.* . . .

Abel
Discourses

Ethical Theories

Friedrich Nietzsche
Beyond Good and Evil
(selection)

© McGraw–Hill, Inc., 1994

119

**287** What is noble? What does the word "noble" still mean for us nowa-days? How does the noble man betray himself, how is he recognised under this heavy overcast sky of the commencing plebeianism, by which every-thing is rendered opaque and leaden? It is not his actions which establish his claim (actions are always ambiguous, always inscrutable); neither is it his "works." One finds nowadays among artists and scholars plenty of those who betray by their works that a profound longing for nobleness impels them; but this very *need of* nobleness is radically different from the needs of the noble soul itself, and is in fact the eloquent and dangerous sign of the lack thereof. It is not the works, but the *belief* which is here decisive and de-termines the order of rank—to employ once more an old religious formula with a new and deeper meaning. It is some fundamental certainty which a noble soul has about itself, something which is not to be sought, is not to be found, and perhaps, also, is not to be lost. *The noble soul has reverence for itself.*

▶ NOTES

1. *désintéressement:* unselfishness (French) [D.C.A., ed.]
2. *raffinement:* refinement (French) [D.C.A.]
3. *un bonhomme:* a simple-minded person; literally, "a good person" (French) [D.C.A.]
4. *gai saber:* the art of the troubadours (a fourteenth-century French term that means, literally, "the merry science") [D.C.A.]
5. *atavism:* recurrence of a trait that appeared in one's remote ancestors [D.C.A.]
6. *inter pares:* among equals (Latin) [D.C.A.]

120

Abel
Discourses

Human Nature and
Ethical Theories

Friedrich Nietzsche
Human, All Too Human
(selection)

© McGraw–Hill, Inc., 1995

# Human, All Too Human

Friedrich Nietzsche

Friedrich Nietzsche was born in Röcken, Prussia, in 1844. After graduating from the Lutheran boarding school at Pforta in 1864, he enrolled in the University of Bonn to study theology. There he began to doubt his Christian faith (he eventually became an atheist and harsh critic of Christianity) and in 1865 transferred to the University of Leipzig to study classical philology (Greek and Latin language and literature) and music. He was recognized as a brilliant student of philology, and at the age of twenty-four, before he had even finished his doctorate, he was offered the chair of classical philology at the University of Basel in Switzerland. The University of Leipzig quickly granted his degree, and Nietzsche assumed the professorship at Basel in 1869. Ten years later, because of his increasingly bad health, Nietzsche resigned his position. For the next ten years, half blind and in unremitting pain, he wandered through Switzerland, Germany, and Italy in search of a cure. His mental health began to deteriorate as well; in 1889 he collapsed on the streets of Turin, Italy, completely insane. He died in Weimar in 1900.

Nietzsche's principal works are *The Birth of Tragedy out of the Spirit of Music* (1872), *Human, All Too Human* (1878), *The Gay Science* (1882), *Thus Spoke Zarathustra* (1883–1885), *Beyond Good and Evil* (1886), and *On the Genealogy of Morals* (1887).

Our selection is from the Second Division of *Human, All Too Human,* entitled "The History of the Moral Sentiments." Nietzsche here presents, in a series of aphorisms, psychological observations on the origin and subsequent history of our notions of good and evil. Placing human nature on "the psychological dissecting table," he analyzes the motivation behind human actions and finds that everything we do—whether "good" or "evil"—stems from a desire to gain pleasure (including the pleasure of exercising power) and avoid pain. No matter how selfless an act may appear, it is ultimately selfish. The fact that our human nature drives us always to seek pleasure and avoid pain means that we have no free will: All actions of human beings, just as those of a waterfall, follow from the necessity of nature. We therefore have no moral responsibility for our actions; neither praise nor blame is warranted. To say that someone is "moral" means simply that he or she follows custom or tradition. Nietzsche concludes by expressing his hope that eventually humankind will transcend morality and produce wise and consciously innocent human beings.

▶ SECOND DIVISION: THE HISTORY
OF THE MORAL SENTIMENTS

35

**Advantages of Psychological Observation** That reflection on the human, all too human (or, according to the learned expression, psychological observation) is one of the means by which one may lighten the burden of life; that exercise in this art produces presence of mind in difficult circumstances, in the midst of tiresome surroundings; even that from the most thorny and unpleasant periods of one's own life one may gather maxims and thereby feel a little better—all this was believed, was known in former

Abel
Discourses

Human Nature and
Ethical Theories

Friedrich Nietzsche
Human, All Too Human
(selection)

© McGraw–Hill, Inc., 1995

121

centuries. Why was it forgotten by our century, when in Germany at least, even in all Europe, the poverty of psychological observation betrays itself by many signs? Not exactly in novels, tales, and philosophical treatises (they are the work of exceptional individuals), rather in the judgments on public events and personalities. But above all there is a lack of the art of psychological analysis and summing-up in every rank of society, in which a great deal is talked about men, but nothing about *man*. Why do we allow the richest and most harmless subject of conversation to escape us? Why are not the great masters of psychological maxims more read? For, without any exaggeration, the educated man in Europe who has read La Rochefoucauld[1] and his kindred in mind and art, is rarely found. And still more rare is he who knows them and does not blame them. . . .

### 36

**Objection**   Or should there be a counterreckoning to that theory that places psychological observation amongst the means of charming, curing, and relieving existence? Should one have sufficiently convinced oneself of the unpleasant consequences of this art to divert from it designedly the attention of him who is educating himself in it? As a matter of fact, a certain blind belief in the goodness of human nature, an innate aversion to the analysis of human actions, a kind of shamefacedness with respect to the nakedness of the soul may really be more desirable for the general well-being of a man than that quality, useful in isolated cases, of psychological sharp-sightedness. And perhaps the belief in goodness, in virtuous men and deeds, in an abundance of impersonal goodwill in the world, has made men better inasmuch as it has made them less distrustful. . . .

### 37

**Nevertheless**   However it may be with reckoning and counter-reckoning, in the present condition of philosophy the awakening of moral observation is necessary. Humanity can no longer be spared the cruel sight of the psychological dissecting-table with its knives and forceps. For here rules that science which inquires into the origin and history of the so-called moral sentiments, and which, in its progress, has to draw up and solve complicated sociological problems. The older philosophy knows the latter one not at all, and has always avoided the examination of the origin and history of moral sentiments on any feeble pretext. With what consequences it is now very easy to see, after it has been shown by many examples how the mistakes of the greatest philosophers generally have their starting-point in a wrong explanation of certain human actions and sensations, just as on the ground of an erroneous analysis—for instance, that of the so-called unselfish actions—a false ethic is built up; then, to harmonise with this again, religion and mythological confusion are brought in to assist; and finally the shades of these dismal spirits fall also over physics and the gener-

**Abel**
**Discourses**

**Human Nature and**
**Ethical Theories**

**Friedrich Nietzsche**
**Human, All Too Human**
**(selection)**

© McGraw–Hill, Inc., 1995

al mode of regarding the world. If it is certain, however, that superficiality in psychological observation has laid, and still lays, the most dangerous snares for human judgments and conclusions, then there is need now of that endurance of work which does not grow weary of piling stone upon stone, pebble on pebble; there is need of courage not to be ashamed of such humble work and to turn a deaf ear to scorn. . . .

**39**

**The Fable of Intelligible Freedom**   The history of the sentiments by means of which we make a person responsible consists of the following principal phases. First, all single actions are called "good" or "bad" without any regard to their motives, but only on account of the useful or injurious consequences which result for the community. But soon the origin of these distinctions is forgotten, and it is deemed that the qualities "good" or "bad" are contained in the action itself without regard to its consequences, by the same error according to which language describes the stone as hard, the tree as green—with which, in short, the *result* is regarded as the *cause*. Then the goodness or badness is implanted in the motive, and the action in itself is looked upon as morally ambiguous. Mankind even goes further and applies the predicate "good" or "bad" no longer to single motives, but to the whole nature of an individual, out of whom the motive grows as the plant grows out of the earth. Thus, in turn, man is made responsible for his operations, then for his actions, then for his motives, and finally for his nature. Eventually it is discovered that even this nature cannot be responsible, inasmuch as it is an absolutely necessary consequence . . . of the elements and influences of past and present things—that man, therefore, cannot be made responsible for anything, neither for his nature, nor his motives, nor his actions, nor his effects. It has therewith come to be recognised that the history of moral valuations is at the same time the history of an error, the error of responsibility, which is based upon the error of the freedom of will. . . . Nobody is responsible for his actions, nobody for his nature; to judge is identical with being unjust. This also applies when an individual judges himself. The theory is as clear as sunlight, and yet everyone prefers to go back into the shadow and the untruth, for fear of the consequences. . . .

**42**

**The Order of Possessions and Morality**   The once-accepted hierarchy of possessions, according as this or the other is coveted by a lower, higher, or highest egoism, now decides what is moral or immoral. To prefer a lesser good (for instance, the gratification of the senses) to a more highly valued good (for instance, health) is accounted immoral, and also to prefer luxury to liberty. The hierarchy of possessions, however, is not fixed and equal at all times; if anyone prefers vengeance to justice he is moral according to the standard of an earlier civilisation, but immoral according to the present one. To be "immoral," therefore, denotes that an individual has not felt, or not felt sufficiently strongly, the higher, finer, spiritual motives which have come in with a new culture; it marks one who has remained behind, but only according to the difference of degrees. The order of possessions itself is *not* raised and lowered according to a moral point of view; but each time that it is fixed it supplies the decision as to whether an action is moral or immoral. . . .

## 44

**Gratitude and Revenge** The reason why the powerful man is grateful is this: his benefactor, through the benefit he confers, has mistaken and intruded into the sphere of the powerful man. Now the latter, in return, penetrates into the sphere of the benefactor by the act of gratitude. It is a milder form of revenge. Without the satisfaction of gratitude, the powerful man would have shown himself powerless, and would have been reckoned as such ever after. Therefore every society of the good (which originally meant the powerful) places gratitude among the first duties. . . .

## 45

**The Twofold Early History of Good and Evil** The conception of good and evil has a twofold early history. [*First,*] in the soul of the ruling tribes and castes. Whoever has the power of returning good for good, evil for evil, and really practises requital, and who is, therefore, grateful and revengeful, is called "good"; whoever is powerless and unable to requite, is reckoned as "bad." As a good man, one is reckoned among the "good," a community which has common feelings because the single individuals are bound to one another by the sense of requital. As a bad man, one belongs to the "bad," to a party of subordinate, powerless people who have no common feeling. The good are a caste; the bad are a mass like dust. "Good" and "bad" have for a long time meant the same thing as noble and base, master and slave. On the other hand, the enemy is not looked upon as evil; he can requite. In Homer,[2] the Trojan and the Greek are both good. It is not the one who injures us, but the one who is despicable, who is called bad. Good is inherited in the community of the good; it is impossible that a bad man could spring from such good soil. If, nevertheless, one of the good ones does something which is unworthy of the good, refuge is sought in excuses. The guilt is thrown upon a god, for instance; it is said that he has struck the good man with blindness and madness.

[*Second,*] in the soul of the oppressed and powerless. Here every *other* man is looked upon as hostile, inconsiderate, rapacious, cruel, cunning, be he noble or base. "Evil" is the distinguishing word for man, even for every conceivable living creature—for example, for a god. "Human," "divine," [mean] the same thing as "devilish," "evil." The signs of goodness, helpfulness, pity, are looked upon with fear as spite, the prelude to a terrible result, stupefaction and outwitting—in short, as refined malice. With such a disposition in the individual, a community could hardly exist; or at most it could exist only in its crudest form, so that in all places where this conception of good and evil obtains, the downfall of the single individuals, of their tribes and races, is at hand. Our present civilisation has grown up on the soil of the *ruling* tribes and castes. . . .

### 56

**Victory of Knowledge over Radical Evil**   It is of great advantage to him who desires to be wise to have witnessed for a time the spectacle of a thoroughly evil and degenerate man; it is false, like the contrary spectacle, but for whole long periods it held the mastery, and its roots have even extended and ramified themselves to us and our world. In order to understand *ourselves* we must understand *it;* but then, in order to mount higher we must rise above it. We recognise, then, that there exist no sins in the metaphysical sense; but, in the same sense, also no virtues; we recognise that the entire domain of ethical ideas is perpetually tottering, that there are higher and deeper conceptions of good and evil, of moral and immoral. He who does not desire much more from things than a knowledge of them easily makes peace with his soul, and will make a mistake (or commit a sin, as the world calls it) at the most from ignorance, but hardly from covetousness. He will no longer wish to excommunicate and exterminate desires; but his only, his wholly dominating, ambition to *know* as well as possible at all times, will make him cool and will soften all the savageness in his disposition. Moreover, he has been freed from a number of tormenting conceptions; he has no more feeling at the mention of the words "punishments of hell," "sinfulness," "incapacity for good"; he recognises in them only the vanishing shadow-pictures of false views of the world and of life.

### 57

**Morality as the Self-Disintegration of Man**   A good author, who really has his heart in his work, wishes that someone could come and annihilate him by representing the same thing in a clearer way and answering without more ado the problems therein proposed. The loving girl wishes she could prove the self-sacrificing faithfulness of her love by the unfaithfulness of her beloved. The soldier hopes to die on the field of battle for his victorious fatherland, for his loftiest desires triumph in the victory of his country. The mother gives to the child that of which she deprives herself: sleep, the best food, sometimes her health and fortune. But are all these unegoistic conditions? Are these deeds of morality *miracles* because, to use Schopenhauer's[3] expression, they are "impossible and yet performed"? Is it not clear that in all four cases the individual loves *something of himself,* a thought, a desire, a production, better than *anything else of himself;* that he therefore divides his nature and to one part sacrifices all the rest? Is it something *entirely* different when an obstinate man says, "I would rather be shot than move a step out of my way for this man"? The *desire for something* (wish, inclination, longing) is present in all the instances mentioned; to give way to it, with all its consequences, is certainly not "unegoistic." In ethics man does not consider himself as *individuum* but as *dividuum*.[4] . . .

### 92

**The Origin of Justice** Justice (equity) has its origin among powers which are fairly equal, as Thucydides (in the terrible dialogue between the Athenian and Melian ambassadors)[5] rightly comprehended. That is to say, where there is no clearly recognisable supremacy, and where a conflict would be useless and would injure both sides, there arises the thought of coming to an understanding and settling the opposing claims; the character of *exchange* is the primary character of justice. Each party satisfies the other, as each obtains what he values more than the other. Each one receives that which he desires, as his own henceforth; and whatever is desired, is received in return. Justice, therefore, is recompense and exchange based on the hypothesis of a fairly equal degree of power. Thus, originally, revenge belongs to the province of justice; it is an exchange. Also gratitude. Justice naturally is based on the point of view of a judicious self-preservation, on the egoism, therefore, of that reflection, "Why should I injure myself uselessly and perhaps not attain my aim after all?" So much about the *origin* of justice. Because man, according to his intellectual custom, has *forgotten* the original purpose of so-called just and reasonable actions, and particularly because for hundreds of years children have been taught to admire and imitate such actions, the idea has gradually arisen that such an action is unegoistic. Upon this idea, however, is based the high estimation in which [such actions are] held—which, moreover, like all valuations, is constantly growing, for something that is valued highly is striven after, imitated, multiplied, and increases, because the value of the output of toil and enthusiasm of each individual is added to the value of the thing itself. How little moral would the world look without this forgetfulness! A poet might say that God had placed forgetfulness as doorkeeper in the temple of human dignity. . . .

### 94

**The Three Phases of Hitherto Existing Morality** It is the first sign that the animal has become man when its actions no longer have regard only to momentary welfare but to what is enduring, when it grows *useful* and *practical;* there the free rule of reason first breaks out. A still higher step is reached when he acts according to the principle of *honour.* By this means he brings himself into order, submits to common feelings, and that exalts him still higher over the phase in which he was led only by the idea of usefulness from a personal point of view; he respects and wishes to be respected—that is, he understands usefulness as dependent upon what he thinks of others and what others think of him. Eventually he acts, on the highest step of the *hitherto* existing morality, according to *his* standard of things and men; he himself decides for himself and others what is honourable, what is useful. He has become the lawgiver of opinions, in accordance with the ever more highly developed idea of what is useful and honourable. Knowledge enables him to place that which is most useful (that is to say, the general), enduring usefulness above the personal; the honourable recognition of general, enduring validity above the momentary. He lives and acts as a collective individual. . . .

## 96

**Custom and Morality**  To be moral, correct, and virtuous is to be obedient to an old-established law and custom. Whether we submit with difficulty or willingly is immaterial; enough that we do so. He is called "good" who, as if naturally, after long precedent (easily and willingly, therefore) does what is right, according to whatever this may be (as, for instance, taking revenge, if to take revenge be considered as right, as among the ancient Greeks). He is called good because he is good "for something." But [because] goodwill, pity, consideration, moderation, and such like, have come, with the change in manners, to be looked upon as "good for something," as useful—[thus] good-natured and helpful [people] have, later on, come to be distinguished specially as "good." (In the beginning other and more important kinds of usefulness stood in the foreground.) To be evil is to be "not moral" (immoral); to be immoral is to be in opposition to tradition, however sensible or stupid it may be. Injury to the community (the "neighbour" being understood thereby) has, however, been looked upon by the social laws of all different ages as being eminently the actual "immorality," so that now at the word "evil" we immediately think of voluntary injury to one's neighbour. The fundamental antithesis which has taught man the distinction between moral and immoral, between good and evil, is not the "egoistic" and "unegoistic," but the being bound to the tradition, law, and [being released from it]. How the tradition has *arisen* is immaterial, at all events without regard to good and evil or any immanent categorical imperative,[6] but above all for the purpose of preserving a *community*, a generation, an association, a people. Every superstitious custom that has arisen on account of some falsely explained accident, creates a tradition which it is moral to follow. To separate one's self from it is dangerous, but more dangerous for the *community* than for the individual (because the Godhead punishes the community for every outrage and every violation of its rights, and the individual only in proportion). Now every tradition grows continually more venerable, the farther off lies its origin, the more this is lost sight of. The veneration paid it accumulates from generation to generation, the tradition at last becomes holy and excites awe;

and thus in any case the morality of piety is a much older morality than that which requires unegoistic actions.

## 97

**Pleasure In Traditional Custom** An important species of pleasure, and therewith the source of morality, arises out of habit. Man does what is habitual to him more easily, better, and therefore more willingly; he feels a pleasure therein, and knows from experience that the habitual has been tested, and is therefore useful. A custom that we can live with is proved to be wholesome and advantageous in contrast to all new and not yet tested experiments. According to this, morality is the union of the pleasant and the useful; moreover, it requires no reflection. As soon as man can use compulsion, he uses it to introduce and enforce his *customs;* for in his eyes they are proved as the wisdom of life. In the same way, a company of individuals compels each single one to adopt the same customs. Here the inference is wrong; because we feel at ease with a morality, or at least because we are able to carry on existence with it, therefore this morality is necessary, for it seems to be the *only* possibility of feeling at ease; the ease of life seems to grow out of it alone. This comprehension of the habitual as a necessity of existence is pursued even to the smallest details of custom. As insight into genuine causality is very small with lower peoples and civilisations, they take precautions with superstitious fear that everything should go in its same groove; even where custom is difficult, hard, and burdensome, it is preserved on account of its apparent highest usefulness. It is not known that the same degree of well-being can also exist with other customs, and that even higher degrees may be attained. We become aware, however, that all customs, even the hardest, grow pleasanter and milder with time, and that the severest way of life may become a habit and therefore a pleasure. . . .

## 99

**The Innocent Side of So-called Evil Actions** All "evil" actions are prompted by the instinct of preservation, or, more exactly, by the desire for pleasure and the avoidance of pain on the part of the individual; thus prompted, but not evil. "To cause pain per se"[7] *does not exist,* except in the brains of philosophers; neither does "to give pleasure per se" (pity in Schopenhauer's meaning). In the social condition *before* the [establishment of the] state, we kill the creature—be it ape or man—who tries to take from us the fruit of a tree when we are hungry and approach the tree, as we would still do with animals in inhospitable countries. The evil actions which now most rouse our indignation are based upon the error that he who causes them has a free will, that he had the option, therefore, of not doing us this injury. This belief in option arouses hatred, desire for revenge, spite, and the deterioration of the whole imagination—while we are much less angry with an animal because we consider it not responsible. To do injury, not from the instinct of preservation, but as *requital,* is the consequence of a false judgment and therefore equally innocent. The individual can, in the condition which lies before the state, act sternly and cruelly towards other creatures for the purpose of *terrifying,* to establish his existence firmly by such terrifying proofs of his power. Thus act the violent, the mighty, the original founders of states, who subdue the weaker to themselves. They have the right to do so, such as the state still takes for itself; or rather, there is no right that can hinder this. The ground for all morality can only be made ready when a stronger individual or a collective individual—for instance society or the state—subdues the single individuals, draws them out of their singleness, and forms them into an association. *Compulsion* precedes morality; indeed, morality itself is compulsion for a time, to which one submits for the avoidance of pain. Later on it becomes custom; later still, free obedience; and finally almost instinct. Then, like everything long accustomed and natural, it is connected with pleasure—and is henceforth called *virtue.* . . .

### 102

**"Man Always Acts Rightly"**[8]   We do not complain of nature as immoral because it sends a thunderstorm and makes us wet; why do we call those who injure us immoral? Because in the latter case we take for granted a free will functioning voluntarily; in the former we see necessity. But this distinction is an error. Thus we do not call even intentional injury immoral in all circumstances. For instance, we kill a fly unhesitatingly and intentionally, only because its buzzing annoys us; we punish a criminal intentionally and hurt him in order to protect ourselves and society. In the first case it is the individual who, in order to preserve himself, or even to protect himself from worry, does intentional injury; in the second case it is the state. All morals allow intentional injury *in the case of necessity*—that is, when it is a matter of *self-preservation.* But these two points of view suffice to explain all evil actions committed by men against men; we are desirous of obtaining pleasure or avoiding pain; in any case, it is always a question of self-preservation. Socrates and Plato are right: whatever man does he always does well, that is, he does that which seems to him good (useful) according to the degree of his intellect, the particular standard of his reasonableness. . . .

### 105

**Recompensing Justice**   Whoever has completely comprehended the doctrine of absolute nonresponsibility can no longer include the so-called punishing and recompensing justice in the idea of justice, should this consist of giving to each man his due. For he who is punished does not deserve the punishment; he is only used as a means of henceforth warning away from certain actions. Equally so, he who is rewarded does not merit this reward;

he could not act otherwise than he did. Therefore the reward is meant only as an encouragement to him and others, to provide a motive for subsequent actions; words of praise are flung to the runners on the course, not to the one who has reached the goal. Neither punishment nor reward is anything that comes to one as *one's own;* they are given from motives of usefulness, without one having a right to claim them. Hence we must say, "The wise man gives no reward because the deed has been well done," just as we have said, "The wise man does not punish because evil has been committed, but in order that evil shall not be committed." If punishment and reward no longer existed, then the strongest motives which deter men from certain actions and impel them to certain other actions would also no longer exist. The needs of mankind require their continuance; and inasmuch as punishment and reward, blame and praise, work [best] on vanity, the same need requires the continuance of vanity.

### 106

**At the Waterfall** In looking at a waterfall, we imagine that there is freedom of will and fancy in the countless turnings, twistings, and breakings of the waves; but everything is compulsory, every movement can be mathematically calculated. So it is also with human actions; one would be able to calculate every single action beforehand if one were all-knowing; equally so, all progress of knowledge, every error, all malice. The one who acts certainly labours under the illusion of voluntariness. If the world's wheel were to stand still for a moment and an all-knowing, calculating reason were there to make use of this pause, it could foretell the future of every creature to the remotest times, and mark out every track upon which that wheel would continue to roll. The delusion of the acting agent about himself (the supposition of a free will) belongs to this mechanism which [is to] be calculated.

### 107

**Nonresponsibility and Innocence** The complete nonresponsibility of man for his actions and his nature is the bitterest drop which he who understands must swallow if he was accustomed to see the [claim to the] nobility of his humanity in responsibility and duty. All his valuations, distinctions, disinclinations, are thereby deprived of value and become false. His deepest feeling for the sufferer and the hero was based on an error; he may no longer either praise or blame, for it is absurd to praise and blame nature and necessity. In the same way as he loves a fine work of art, but does not praise it, because it can do nothing for itself; in the same way as he regards plants—so must he regard his own actions and those of mankind. He can admire strength, beauty, abundance, in themselves—but must find no merit therein. The chemical progress and the strife of the elements, the torments of the sick person who thirsts after recovery—are all equally as little merits as those struggles of the soul and states of distress in which we are torn hither and thither by different impulses until we finally decide for the strongest, as we say (but in reality it is the strongest motive which decides for us). All these motives, however (whatever fine names we may give them), have all grown out of the same root, in which we believe the evil poisons to be situated; between good and evil actions there is no difference of species, but at most of degree. Good actions are sublimated evil ones; evil actions are vulgarised and stupefied good ones. The single longing of the individual for self-gratification (together with the fear of losing it) satisfies itself in all circumstances: man may act as he can, that is, as he must, be it in deeds of vanity, revenge, pleasure, usefulness, malice, cunning; be it in deeds of sacrifice, of pity, of knowledge. The degrees of the power of judgment determine [where] anyone lets himself be drawn through this longing. To every society, to every individual, a scale of possessions is continually present, according to which he determines his actions and judges those of others. But this standard changes constantly; many actions are called evil and are only stupid, because the degree of intelligence which decided for them was very low. In a certain sense, even, *all* actions are still stupid; for the highest degree of human intelligence which can now be attained will assuredly be yet surpassed, and then, in a retrospect, all our actions and judgments will appear as limited and hasty as the actions and judgments of primitive wild peoples now appear limited and hasty to us. To recognise all this may be deeply painful, but consolation comes after: such pains are the pangs of birth. The butterfly wants to break through its chrysalis: it rends and tears it, and is then blinded and confused by the unaccustomed light, the kingdom of liberty. In such people as are *capable* of such sadness—and how few are!—the first experiment made is to see whether *mankind can change itself* from a *moral* into a *wise* mankind. The sun of a new gospel throws its rays upon the highest point in the soul of each single individual, then the mists gather thicker than ever, and the brightest light and the dreariest shadow lie side by side. Everything is necessity—so says the new knowledge, and this knowledge itself is necessity. Everything is innocence, and knowledge is the road to insight into this innocence. Were pleasure, egoism, vanity *necessary* for the production of the moral phenomena and their highest result, the sense for truth and justice in knowledge; were error and the confusion of the imagination the only means through which mankind could raise itself gradually to this degree of self-enlightenment and self-liberation—who would dare to undervalue these means? Who would dare to be sad if he perceived the goal to which those roads led? Everything in the domain of morality has evolved, is changeable, unstable; everything is dissolved, it is true. But *everything is also streaming towards one goal.* Even if the inherited habit of erroneous valuation, love and hatred, continue to reign in us, yet under the influence of growing knowledge it will become weaker. A new habit, that of comprehension, of not loving, not hating, of overlooking, is gradually implanting itself

Abel
Discourses

Human Nature and
Ethical Theories

Friedrich Nietzsche
Human, All Too Human
(selection)

© McGraw–Hill, Inc., 1995

131

in us upon the same ground, and in thousands of years will perhaps be powerful enough to give humanity the strength to produce wise, innocent (consciously innocent) men, as it now produces unwise, guilt conscious men—*that is the necessary preliminary step, not its opposite.*

---

▶ NOTES

1. Duc François de La Rochefoucauld (1613–1680) was a French moralist and writer of aphorisms. [D.C.A., ed.]

2. Homer (8th or 9th century B.C.E.) is the Greek poet to whom the epics the *Iliad* and the *Odyssey* are attributed. The *Iliad* deals with the war between the Greeks and the Trojans. [D.C.A.]

3. Arthur Schopenhauer (1788–1860) was a German philosopher. [D.C.A.]

4. *Individuum* is Latin for "an undivided thing"; *dividuum* means "a divided thing." [D.C.A.]

5. Thucydides (about 460–400 B.C.E.) was a Greek historian. His account of the conversation between the ambassadors of Athens and Melos appears in his *History of the Peloponnesian War,* Book V, sections 84–113. The Athenians enslaved the Melians in 416. [D.C.A.]

6. *categorical imperative:* an unconditionally binding moral obligation [D.C.A.]

7. *per se:* of and by itself (Latin) [D.C.A.]

8. A paraphrase of the view defended by Socrates in Plato, *Gorgias,* Stephanus p. 468. [D.C.A.]